# THE PSYCHOLOGY OF MAN'S POSSIBLE EVOLUTION

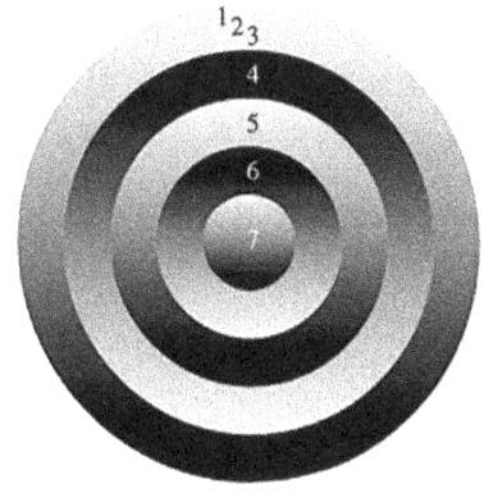


P. D. OUSPENSKY

*First published c.1947*

*With*

Notes On Decision To Work

Notes On Work On Oneself

What Is School?

First published 2018 by Aziloth Books




British Library Cataloguing in Publication Data

A catalogue record for this book is available from the British Library

ISBN-13: 978-1-911405-62-7

Illustrations:

Front cover: *Developing Broad Bean (Vicia faba)*

Title page: *Division of Man into Seven Categories or Stages of Development*

# CONTENTS

# INTRODUCTION

Some years ago I began to receive letters from readers of my books. All these letters contained one question, *what I had been doing after I had written my books*, which were published in English in 1920 and 1931, and had been written in 1910 and 1912.

I could never answer these letters. It would have needed books, even to attempt to do this. But when the people who wrote to me lived in London, where I lived after 1921, I invited them and arranged courses of lectures for them. In these lectures I tried to answer their questions and explain what I had discovered after I had written my two books, and what was the direction of my work.

In 1934 I wrote five preliminary lectures which gave a general idea of what I was studying, and also of the lines along which a certain number of people were working with me. To put all that in one, or even in two or three lectures, was quite impossible: so I always warned people that it was not worth while hearing one lecture, or two, but that only five, or better ten lectures could give an idea of the direction of my work. These lectures have continued since then, and throughout this time I have often corrected and rewritten them.

On the whole I found the general arrangement satisfactory. Five lectures were read, in my presence or without me; listeners could ask questions; and if they tried to follow the advice and indications given them, which referred chiefly to self-observation and a certain self-discipline, they very soon had a quite sufficient working understanding of what I was doing.

I certainly recognised all the time that five lectures were not sufficient, and in talks that followed them I elaborated and enlarged the preliminary data, trying to show people their own position in relation to the *New Knowledge*.

I found that the chief difficulty for most people was to realise that they had really heard *new things*, that is, things that they had never heard before.

They did not formulate it for themselves, but in fact they always tried to contradict this in their minds and translate what they heard into their habitual language, whatever it happened to be. And this certainly I could not take into account.

I know that it is not an easy thing to realize that one is hearing *new things*. We are so accustomed to the old tunes, and the old motives, that long ago we ceased to hope and ceased to believe that there might be anything new.

And when we hear new things, we take them for old, or think that they can be explained and interpreted by the old. It is true that it is a difficult task to realize the possibility and necessity of quite new ideas, and it needs with time a revaluation of all usual values.

I cannot guarantee that you will hear new ideas, that is, ideas you never heard before, from the start; but if you are patient you will very soon begin to notice them. And then I wish you not to miss them, and to try not to interpret them in the old way.

*New York, 1945*

# FIRST LECTURE

I shall speak about the study of psychology, but I must warn you that the psychology about which I speak is very different from anything you may know under this name.

To begin with I must say that practically never in history has psychology stood at *so low a level* as at the present time. It has lost all touch with its *origin* and its *meaning* so that now it is even difficult to define the term psychology: that is, to say what psychology is and what it studies. And this is so in spite of the fact that never in history have there been so many psychological theories and so many psychological writings.

Psychology is sometimes called a new science. This is quite wrong. Psychology is, perhaps, the *oldest science*, and, unfortunately, in its most essential features a *forgotten science*.

In order to understand how psychology can be defined it is necessary to realise that psychology except in modern times has never existed under its own name. For one reason or another psychology always was suspected of *wrong or subversive tendencies*, either religious or political or moral and had to use different disguises.

For thousands of years psychology existed under the name of philosophy. In India all forms of *Yoga*, which are essentially psychology, are described as one of the six systems of philosophy. *Sufi teachings*, which again are chiefly psychological, are regarded as partly religious and partly metaphysical. In Europe, even quite recently in the last decades of the nineteenth century, many works on psychology were referred to as philosophy. And in spite of the fact that almost all sub-divisions of philosophy such as logic, the theory of cognition, ethics, aesthetics, referred to the work of the human mind or senses, psychology was regarded as inferior to philosophy and as relating only to the lower or more trivial sides of human nature.

Parallel with its existence under the name of philosophy, psychology existed even longer connected with one or another religion. It does not mean that religion and psychology ever were one and the same thing, or that the fact of the connection between religion and psychology was recognised. But there is no doubt that almost every known religion – certainly I do not mean modern *sham religions* – developed one or another kind of psychological teaching connected often with a certain practice, so that the study of religion very often included in itself the study of psychology.

There are many excellent works on psychology in quite orthodox religious literature of different countries and epochs. For instance, in early Christianity there was a collection of books of different authors under the general name of *Philokalia*, used in our time in the Eastern Church, especially for the instruction of monks.

During the time when psychology was connected with philosophy and religion it also existed in the form of art. Poetry, drama, sculpture, dancing, even architecture, were means for transmitting psychological knowledge. For instance, the Gothic Cathedrals were in their chief meaning works on psychology.

In the ancient times before philosophy, religion and art had taken their separate forms as we now know them, psychology had existed in the form of *Mysteries*, such as those of Egypt and of ancient Greece.

Later, after the disappearance of the Mysteries, psychology existed in the form of *Symbolical Teachings* which were sometimes connected with the religion of the period and sometimes not connected, such as astrology, alchemy, magic, and the more modern: Masonry, occultism and Theosophy.

And here it is necessary to note that all psychological systems and doctrines, those that exist or existed openly and those that were hidden or disguised, can be divided into two chief categories.

First: systems which study man *as they find him, or such as they suppose or imagine him to be*. Modern "scientific" psychology or what is known under that name belongs to this category.

Second: systems which study man not from the point of view of what he is, or what he seems to be, but from the point of view of what he may become; that is, from the point of view of *his possible evolution*.

These last systems are in reality the original ones, or in any case the oldest and only they can explain the forgotten origin and the meaning of psychology.

When we understand the importance of the study of man from the point of view of *his possible evolution*, we shall understand that the first answer to the question: what is psychology? – should be that psychology is the study of the principles, laws and facts of man's possible evolution.

Here, in these lectures, I shall speak only from this point of view.

Our first question will be – what does evolution of man mean, and second, are there any special conditions necessary for it?

As regards ordinary modern views on the origin of

man and his previous evolution I must say at once that they cannot be accepted. We must realise that we know nothing about the origin of man and we have no proof of man's physical or mental evolution.

On the contrary, if we take historical mankind, that is, humanity for ten or fifteen thousand years, we may find unmistakable signs of a higher type of man, whose presence can be established on the evidence of ancient monuments and memorials which cannot be repeated or imitated by the present humanity.

As regards *prehistoric man* or creatures similar in appearance to man and yet at the same time very different from him, whose bones are sometimes found in deposits of glacial or pre-glacial periods, we may accept the quite possible view that these bones belong to some being quite different from man, which died out long ago.

Denying previous evolution of man we must deny any possibility of future *mechanical* evolution of man; that is, evolution happening by itself according to laws of heredity and selection, and without man's conscious efforts and understanding of his possible evolution.

Our fundamental idea shall be that man as we know him *is not a completed being*; that nature develops him only up to a certain point and then leaves him, either to develop further, *by his own efforts* and devices, or to live and die such as he was born, or to degenerate and lose capacity for development.

Evolution of man in this case will mean the development of certain *inner* qualities and features which usually remain undeveloped, *and cannot develop by themselves.*

Experience and observation show that this development is possible only in certain definite conditions, with efforts of a certain kind on the part of man himself, and with *sufficient help* from those who began similar work before and have already attained a certain degree of development, *or at least* a certain knowledge of methods.

We must start with the idea that without efforts evolution is impossible; without help, it is also impossible.

After this we must understand that in the way of development, man must become *a different being,* and we must learn and understand in what sense and in which direction man must become a different being; that is, what a different being means.

Then we must understand that *all men* cannot develop and become different beings. Evolution is the question of personal efforts and in relation to the mass of humanity evolution is the rare exception. It may sound strange but we must realise that it is not only rare, *but is becoming more and more rare.*

Many questions naturally arise from the preceding statements: –

> What does it mean that in the way of evolution man must become a different being?
>
> What does "different being" mean?
>
> Which inner qualities or features can be developed in man and how can this be done?
>
> Why cannot all men develop and become different beings?
>
> Why such an injustice?

I shall try to answer these questions and I shall begin with the last one.

Why cannot all men develop and become different beings?

The answer is very simple. *Because they do not want it.*

Because they do not know about it and will not understand without a long preparation what it means, even if they are told.

The chief idea is that in order to become *a different being* man must want it very much and for a very long time. A passing desire or a vague desire based on dissatisfaction with external conditions will not create a sufficient impulse.

The evolution of man depends on his understanding of what he may get and what he must give for it.

If man does not want it, or if he does not want it *strongly enough*, and does not make necessary efforts, he will never develop. So there is no injustice in this. Why should man have what he does not want? If man were forced to become a different being when he is satisfied with what he is, then this would be injustice.

Now we must ask ourselves what a *different being* means. If we consider all the material we can find that refers to this question, we find an assertion that in becoming a different being man acquires many new qualities and powers which he does not possess now. This is a common assertion which we find in all kinds of systems admitting the idea of psychological or inner growth of man.

But this is not sufficient. Even the most detailed descriptions of these new powers will not help us in any way to understand how they appear and where they come from.

There is a missing link in ordinary known theories, even in those I already mentioned which are based on the idea of the possibility of evolution of man.

The truth lies in the fact that before acquiring any *new* faculties or powers which man does not know and does not possess now, he must acquire faculties and powers he *also does not possess*, but which he ascribes to himself; that is, he thinks that he knows them and can use and control them.

This is the missing link, and *this is the most important point.*

By way of evolution, as described before, that is, a way based on effort and help, man must acquire qualities which he thinks he already possesses, but about which he deceives himself.

In order to understand this better, and to know what are these faculties and powers which man can acquire, both quite new and unexpected and also those which he imagines that he already possesses, we must begin with man's general knowledge about himself.

And here we come at once to a very important fact.

*Man does not know himself.*

He does not know his own limitations and his own possibilities. He does not even know to how great an extent he does not know himself.

Man has invented many machines, and he knows that a complicated machine needs sometimes years of careful study before one can use it or control it. But he does not apply this knowledge to himself, although he himself is a much more complicated machine than any machine he has invented.

He has all sorts of wrong ideas about himself. First of all he does not realise that he *actually is a machine.*

What does it mean that man is a machine?

It means that he has no independent movements, inside or outside of himself. He is a machine which is brought into motion by *external influences and external impacts.* All his movements, actions, words, ideas, emotions, moods and thoughts are produced by external influences. By himself, he is just an automaton with a certain store of memories of previous experiences, and a certain amount of reserve energy.

*We must understand that man can do nothing.*

But he does not realise this and ascribes to himself the *capacity to do*. This is the first wrong thing that man ascribes to himself.

That must be understood very clearly. *Man cannot do.* Everything that man thinks he does, really *happens*. It happens exactly as "it rains," or "it thaws."

In the English language there are no impersonal verbal forms which can be used in relation to human actions. So we must continue to say that man thinks, reads, writes, loves, hates, starts wars, fights, and so on. Actually, all this *happens.*

Man cannot move, think or speak of his own accord. He is a marionette pulled here and there by invisible strings. If he understands this, he can learn more about himself, and possibly then things may begin to change for him. But if he cannot realise and understand his *utter mechanicalness* or if he does not wish to accept it as a fact, he can learn nothing more, and things cannot change for him.

*Man is a machine,* but a very peculiar machine. He is a machine which, in right circumstances, and with right treatment, *can know that he is a machine*, and having fully realised this, he may find the ways to cease to be a machine.

First of all, what man must know is that he is not one; he is many. He has not one permanent and unchangeable "I" or Ego. He is always different. One moment he is one, another moment he is another, the third moment he is a third, and so on, almost without an end.

The illusion of unity or oneness is created in man first, by the sensation of one physical body, by *his name*, which in normal cases always remains the same, and third, by a number of mechanical habits which are implanted in him by education or acquired by imitation. Having always the same physical sensations, hearing always the same name and noticing in himself the same habits and inclinations he had before, he believes himself to be always the same.

In reality there is no oneness in man and there is no controlling centre, no permanent "I" or Ego.

This is the general picture of man:

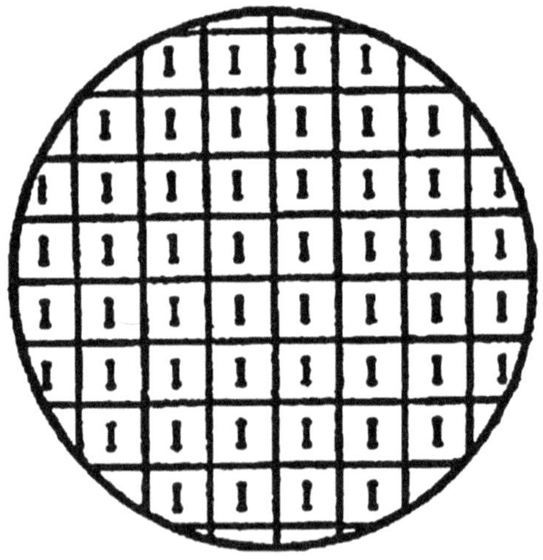

Every thought, every feeling, every sensation, every desire, every like and every dislike is an "I." These "I"s are not connected and are not coordinated in any way. Each of them depends on the change in external circumstances, and on the change of impressions.

Some of them mechanically follow some other, and some appear always accompanied by others. But there is no order and no system in that.

There are certain groups of "I"s which are naturally connected. We will speak about these groups later. Now, we must try to understand that there are groups of "I"s connected only by accidental associations, accidental memories, or quite imaginary similarities.

Each of these "I"s represents at every given moment a very small part of our "brain," "mind," or "intelligence," but each of them means itself to represent *the whole*. When man says "I" it sounds as if he meant the whole of himself, but really even when he himself thinks that he means it, it is only a passing thought, a passing mood, or passing desire. In an hour's time he may completely forget it, and with the same conviction express an opposite opinion, opposite view, opposite interests. The worst of it is that man does not remember it. In most cases he believes in the last "I"which expressed itself, as long as it lasts: that is, as long as another "I" – sometimes quite unconnected with the preceding one – does not express its opinion or its desire louder than the first.

Now let us return to two other questions:

What does development mean? And what does it mean that man can become a different being? Or, in other words, what kind of change is *possible* in man, and how and *when* does this change begin?

It has already been said that the change will begin with those powers and capacities which man *ascribes to himself,* but which, in reality, he does not possess.

This means that before man can acquire any *new* powers

and capacities, he must actually develop in himself those qualities which he *thinks* he possesses, and about which he has the greatest possible illusions.

Development cannot begin on the basis of lying to oneself, or deceiving oneself. Man must know what he has and what he has not. It means that he must realize that he does not possess the qualities already described, which he ascribes to himself; that is, *capacity to do*, *individuality*, or *unity*, *permanent* Ego, and in addition *Consciousness* and *Will*.

It is necessary for man to know this, because as long as he believes that he possesses these qualities he will not make right efforts to acquire them, exactly as a man will not buy costly things and pay a high price for them, if he thinks he already possesses them.

The most important and the most misleading of these qualities is consciousness. And the change in man begins with the change in his understanding of the *meaning of consciousness* and after that with his gradual acquiring command over it.

What is consciousness?

In most cases in ordinary language the word "consciousness" is used as an equivalent to the word "intelligence" in the sense of *mind activity*.

In reality consciousness is a particular kind of "awareness" in man independent from mind's activity – first of all, *awareness of himself*, of *who he is*, *where he is*, and further, awareness of what he knows, of what he does not know, and so on.

Only man himself can know whether he is "conscious" at a given moment or not. This was proven long ago in a certain line of thought in European psychology which understood that only man himself can know certain things in relation to himself.

Applied to the question of consciousness it means that only man himself can know if his consciousness exists at the moment or not. That means that the presence or absence of consciousness in man cannot be proven by observation of his external actions. As I said, this fact was established long ago, but the importance of it was never fully understood because it was always connected with the understanding of consciousness as mental process or mind activity. If man realises that up to the moment of this realisation he was not conscious, and then forgets this realisation – or even remembers it – this is not consciousness. It is only memory of a strong realisation.

Now I want to draw your attention to another fact which has been missed by all modern psychological schools.

It is the fact that the consciousness in man, whatever it means, never remains in the same state. It is either there or not. The highest moments of consciousness create *memory*. Other moments man simply does not remember. This more than anything else produces in man the illusion of continuous consciousness or continuous awareness.

Some of the modern schools of psychology deny consciousness altogether, deny even the necessity of such a term, but this is simply an extravagance of misapprehension. Other schools – if they can be called by this name – speak about *states of consciousness* – meaning thoughts, feelings, moving impulses and sensations. This is based on the fundamental mistake of mixing consciousness with psychic functions. About that we will speak later.

In reality modern thought in most cases still relies on the old formulation, that *consciousness has no degrees*.

General, although tacit, acceptance of this idea, even though it contradicted many later discoveries, stopped many possible observations of variations of consciousness.

The fact is that consciousness has quite visible and observable degrees, *certainly visible and observable in oneself.*

First, there is duration: *How long* one was conscious.

Second, frequency of appearance: *how often* one became conscious.

Third, the extent and penetration: *of what one was conscious*, which can vary very much with the growth of man.

It we take only the first two, we will be able to understand the idea of possible evolution of consciousness. This idea is connected with the most important fact very well known by old psychological schools, like for instance authors of *Philokalia*, but completely missed by European philosophy and psychology of the last two or three centuries.

This is the fact that consciousness can be made continuous and controllable by special efforts and special study.

I shall try to explain how consciousness can be studied. Take a watch and look at the second hand, *trying to be aware of yourself,* and concentrating on the thought, "I am Peter Ouspensky," "I am now here." Try not to think about anything else, simply follow the movements of the second hand and be aware of yourself, your name, your existence and the place where you are. Keep all other thoughts away.

You will, if you are persistent, be able to do this *for two minutes. This is the limit of your consciousness*. And if you try to repeat the experiment soon after, you will find it more difficult than the first time.

This experiment shows that a man, in his natural state,

can with great effort be conscious of *one subject* (himself) for two minutes or less.

The most important deduction one can make after making this experiment in the right way is *that man is not conscious of himself.* The illusion of his being conscious of himself is created by memory and thought processes.

For instance, a man goes to a theatre. If he is accustomed to it, he is not especially conscious of being there while he is there, although he can see things and observe them, enjoy the performance or dislike it, remember it, remember people he met and so on.

When he comes home he remembers that he was in the theatre, and certainly he thinks that he was conscious while he was there. So he has no doubts about his consciousness and he does not realise that his consciousness can be completely absent while he still can act reasonably, think, observe.

For general description, man has possibility of four states of consciousness. They are: *sleep, waking state, self-consciousness and objective consciousness.*

But although he has the possibility of these four states of consciousness, man actually lives only in *two states.* One part of his life passes in sleep, and the other part in what is called "waking state," though in reality his waking state differs very little from sleep.

In ordinary life, man knows nothing of "objective consciousness" and no experiments in this direction are possible. The third state or "self-consciousness" man ascribes to himself; that is, he believes he possesses it, although actually he can be conscious of himself only in very rare flashes and even then he probably does not recognise it because he does not know what it would imply if he actually possessed it. These glimpses of consciousness come in exceptional moments, in highly emotional states, in moments of danger, in very new and unexpected circumstances and situations; or sometimes in quite ordinary moments when nothing in particular happens. But in his ordinary or "normal" state, man has no control over them whatever.

As regards our ordinary memory or moments of memory, we actually *remember* only moments of consciousness, although we do not realise that this is so.

What memory means in a technical sense, and different kinds of memory we possess, I shall explain later. Now I simply want you to turn your attention to your own observations of your memory. You will notice that you remember things differently. Some things you remember quite vividly, some very vaguely and some you do not remember at all. *You only know that they happened.*

You will be very astonished when you realise how little you actually remember. And it happens in this way because you *remember* only the *moments when you were conscious.*

So, in reference to the *third state of consciousness,* we can say that man has occasional moments of self-consciousness leaving vivid memories of circumstances accompanying them but he has no command over them. They come and go by themselves, being controlled by external circumstances, and occasional associations or memories of emotions.

The question arises: Is it possible to acquire command over these fleeting moments of consciousness, to evoke them more often, and to keep them longer, or even make them permanent? In other words, *is it possible to become conscious?*

This is the most important point, and it must be

understood at the very beginning of our study that this point even as a theory has been entirely missed by all modem psychological schools *without an exception.*

For with right methods and the right efforts man *can acquire control of consciousness,* and *can become conscious of himself* with all that it implies. And what it implies we in our present state do not even imagine.

Only after this point has been understood does serious study of psychology become possible.

This study must begin with the investigation of obstacles to consciousness in ourselves, because consciousness can only begin to grow when at least some of these obstacles are removed.

In the following lectures, I shall speak about these obstacles, the greatest of which is *our ignorance of ourselves,* and our wrong conviction that we know ourselves at least to a certain extent and can be sure of ourselves, when in reality we do not know ourselves at all and cannot be sure of ourselves even in *smallest things.*

We must understand now that psychology really means *self-study.* This is the second definition of psychology.

One cannot study psychology as one can study astronomy; that is, apart from oneself.

And at the same time one must study oneself as one studies any new and complicated machine. One must know the parts of this machine, its chief functions, the conditions of right work, the causes of wrong work, and many other things which are difficult to describe without using a special language, which it is also necessary to know in order to be able to study the machine.

The human machine has seven different functions:

1. Thinking (or intellect).
2. Feeling (or emotions).
3. Instinctive function (all inner work of the organism).
4. Moving function (all outer work of the organism, movement in space, and so on).
5. Sex (the function of two principles, male and female, in all their manifestations).

Besides these there are two more functions for which we have no name in ordinary language and which appear only in higher states of consciousness; one – *higher emotional function*, which appears in the *state of self-consciousness*, and the other, *higher mental function*, which appears in the *state of objective consciousness*. As we are not in these states of consciousness we cannot study these functions or experiment with them, and we learn about them only indirectly from those who have attained or experienced them.

In the religious and philosophical literature of different nations there are many allusions to the higher states of consciousness and to higher functions. What creates an additional difficulty in understanding these allusions is the lack of division between the higher states of consciousness. What is called *samadhi* or *ecstatic state or illumination*, or, in more recent works "cosmic consciousness," may refer to one and may refer to another – sometimes to experiences of self-consciousness and sometimes to experiences of objective consciousness. And strange though it may seem we have more material for judging about the highest state; that is, *objective consciousness*, than about the intermediate state; that is, *self-consciousness*, although the former may come only *after* the latter.

Self-study must begin with the study of the four functions; thinking, feeling, instinctive function and moving function. Sex functions can be studied only much later; that is, when these four functions are already sufficiently understood. Contrary to some modern theories the sex function is really posterior; that is, it appears later in life when the first four functions are already fully manifested and is *conditioned by them*. Therefore, the study of the sex function can be useful only when the first four functions are fully known in all their manifestations. At the same time it must be understood that any serious irregularity or abnormality in the sex function makes self-development and even *self-study* impossible.

So now we must try to understand the four chief functions.

I will take it for granted that it is clear to you what I mean by the intellectual or *thinking function*. All mental processes are included here: realisation of an impression, formation of representations and concepts, reasoning, comparison, affirmation, negation, formation of words, speech, imagination, and so on.

The second function is feeling or emotions: joy, sorrow, fear, astonishment, and so on. Even if you are sure that it is clear to you how, and in what manner emotions differ from thoughts I should advise you to verify all your views in regard to this. We mix thought and feelings in our ordinary thinking and speaking; but for the beginning of self-study it is necessary to know clearly which is which.

The two functions following, *instinctive* and *moving*, will take longer to understand, because in no system of Ordinary psychology are these functions described and divided in the right way.

The words "instinct," "instinctive" are generally used in the wrong sense and very often in no sense at all. In particular, to instinct are generally ascribed external functions which are in reality moving functions, and sometimes emotional.

The *Instinctive function* in man includes in itself four different classes of functions:

*First*: All the inner work of the organism, *all physiology* so to speak; digestion and assimilation of food, breathing, circulation of the blood, all the work of inner organs, the building of new cells, the elimination of worked out materials, the work of glands of inner secretion, and so on.

*Second*: The so-called five senses: sight, hearing, smell, taste, touch, and all other senses such as the sense of weight, of temperature, of dryness or of moisture, and so on; that is, all *indifferent* sensations – sensations which by themselves are neither pleasant nor unpleasant.

*Third*: All physical emotions, that is, all physical sensations which are either *pleasant or unpleasant*. All kinds of pain or unpleasant feeling such as unpleasant taste or unpleasant smell, and all kinds of physical pleasure, such as pleasant taste, pleasant smell and so on.

*Fourth*: All reflexes, even the most complicated, such as laughter and yawning; all kinds of physical memory such as memory of taste, memory of smell, memory of pain, which are in reality inner reflexes.

*The moving function* includes in itself all external movements, such as walking, writing, speaking, eating and memories of them. To the moving function also belong those movements which in ordinary language are called "instinctive," such as catching a falling object without thinking. The difference between the instinctive and the moving function is very clear and can be easily understood if one simply remembers that all instinctive functions without exception are inherent and that there is no necessity to learn them in order to use them; whereas on the other hand, none of the moving functions are inherent and one has to learn them all as a child learns to walk, or as one learns to write or to draw. Besides these normal moving functions, there are also some strange moving functions which represent useless work of the human machine not intended by nature, but which occupy a very large place in man's life and use a great quantity of his energy. These are: formation of dreams, imagination, day-dreaming, talking with oneself, all talking for talking's sake, and generally, *all uncontrolled and uncontrollable manifestations.*

The four functions – intellectual, emotional, instinctive and moving – must first be understood in all their manifestations and later they must be observed in oneself. Such self-observation, that is, observation on the right basis, with a preliminary understanding of the states of consciousness and of different functions, constitutes the basis of self-study; that is, *the beginning of psychology.*

It is very important to remember that in observing different functions it is useful to observe at the same time their relation to different states of consciousness.

Let us take the three states of consciousness – sleep, waking state, and possible glimpses of self-consciousness, and the four functions – thinking, feeling, instinctive and moving. All four functions can manifest themselves in sleep, but their manifestations are desultory and unreliable; they cannot be used in any way, they just go by themselves. In the state of waking consciousness or relative consciousness, they can to a certain extent serve for our orientation. Their results can be compared, verified, straightened out, and although they may create many illusions, still in our ordinary state we have nothing else and must make of them what we can. If we knew the quantity of wrong observations, wrong theories, wrong deductions and conclusions made in this state, we should cease to believe ourselves altogether. But men do not realise how deceptive their observations and their theories can be and they continue to believe in them. It is this that keeps man from observing the rare moments when their functions manifest themselves in connection with glimpses of the third state of consciousness; that is, of self-consciousness. All this means that each of the four functions can manifest itself in each of the three states of consciousness. But the results are quite different. When we learn to observe these results and their difference, we shall understand the right relation between functions and states of consciousness.

But before even considering the difference in function in relation to states of consciousness, it is necessary to understand that man's consciousness and man's functions are quite different phenomena, of quite different nature and depending on different causes and that one can exist without the other. *Functions can exist without consciousness and consciousness can exist without functions.*

## SECOND LECTURE

Continuing our study of man, we must now speak with more detail about the different states of consciousness.

As I have already said, there are four states of consciousness possible for man: Sleep, waking consciousness, self-consciousness and objective consciousness; but he lives only in two: partly in sleep and partly in what is sometimes called waking consciousness. It is as though he had a four-storied house, but lived only in the two lower stories.

The first, or the lowest state of consciousness, is *sleep.* This is a purely subjective and passive state. Man is surrounded by dreams. All his psychic functions work without any direction. There is no logic, no sequence, no cause and no result in dreams. Purely subjective pictures – either reflections of former experiences or reflections of vague perceptions of the moment, such as sounds reaching the sleeping man, sensations coming from body, slight pains, sensations of muscular tension – fly through the mind, leaving only a very slight trace on the memory and more often, leaving no trace at all.

The second degree of consciousness comes when man awakes. This second state, the state in which we are now, that is, in which we work, talk, imagine ourselves conscious beings, and so forth, we often call *waking consciousness* or *clear consciousness* but really it should be called "waking sleep" or "relative consciousness." This last term will be explained later.

It is necessary to understand here that the first state of consciousness, that is, sleep, does not disappear when the second state arrives, that is, when man awakes. Sleep remains there, with all its dreams and impressions, only a more critical attitude towards one's own impressions, more connected thoughts, more disciplined actions become added to it, and because of the vividness of sense impressions, desires and feelings – particularly the feeling of *contradiction* or *impossibility*, which is entirely absent in sleep – dreams become invisible exactly as the stars and moon become invisible in the glare of the sun. But they are all there, and they often influence all our thoughts, feelings and actions – sometimes even more than the actual perceptions of the moment.

In connection with this I must say at once that I do not mean what is called in modern psychology "the subconscious" or the "subconscious mind." These are simply wrong expressions, wrong terms, which mean nothing and do not refer to any real facts. There is nothing permanently subconscious in us because there is nothing permanently conscious; and there is no "subconscious mind" for the very simple reason that there is no "conscious mind." Later you will see how this mistake occurred and how this wrong terminology came into being, and became almost generally accepted.

But let us return to the states of consciousness which really exist. The first is sleep. The second is "waking sleep" or "relative consciousness."

The first, as I have said, is a purely subjective state. The second is less subjective; man already distinguishes "I" and "not I" in the sense of his body and objects different from his body, and he can, to a certain extent, orientate among them and know their position and qualities. But it cannot be said that man is awake in this state, because he is very strongly influenced by dreams, and really lives more in dreams than in fact. All the absurdities and all the contradictions of people, and of human life in general, become explained when we realise that people *live in sleep*, do everything in sleep, and do not know that they *are asleep*.

It is useful to remember that this is the inner meaning of many ancient doctrines. The best known to us is Christianity, or the *Gospel teaching*, in which, the idea that men live in sleep and must first of all awake, is the basis of all the explanations of human life, although it is very rarely understood as it should be understood, in this case literally.

But the question is, *how* can a man awake?

The Gospel teaching demands awakening, but does not say how to awaken.

But the psychological study of consciousness shows that only when a man realises that he is asleep, is it possible to say that he is on the way to awakening. He never can awaken without first realising his sleep.

These two states, sleep and waking sleep, are the only two states of consciousness in which man lives. Besides them there are two states of consciousness possible for man, but they become accessible to a man only after a hard and prolonged struggle.

These two higher states of consciousness are called "self-consciousness" and "objective consciousness."

We generally think that we possess self-consciousness, that is, that we are conscious of ourselves, or in any case that we can be conscious of ourselves, at any moment we wish, but in truth "self-consciousness" is a state which *we ascribe to ourselves without any right*. "Objective consciousness" is a state about which we know nothing.

Self consciousness is a state in which man becomes objective towards himself, and objective consciousness is a state in which he comes into contact with the real, or objective world from which he is now shut off by the senses, dreams and subjective states of consciousness.

Another definition of the four states of consciousness can be made from the point of view of the possible *cognition of truth.*

In the first state of consciousness, that is, in sleep, we cannot know anything of the truth. Even if some real perceptions or feelings come to us, they become mixed with dreams, and in the state of sleep we cannot distinguish between dreams and reality.

In the second state of consciousness, that is, in waking sleep, we can only know *relative* truth, and from this comes the term relative consciousness.

In the third state of consciousness, that is, the state of self-consciousness, we can know the full truth *about ourselves.*

In the fourth state of consciousness, that is, in the state of *objective consciousness*, we are supposed to be able to know the full truth *about everything:* we can study "things in themselves," "the world as it is."

This is so far from us that we cannot even think about it in the right way, and we must try to understand that even glimpses of objective consciousness can only come in the fully developed state of self-consciousness.

In the state of sleep we can have glimpses of relative consciousness. In the state of relative consciousness we can have glimpses of self-consciousness. But if we want to have more prolonged periods of self-consciousness and not merely glimpses, we must understand that they cannot come by themselves, they need *will action.* This means that frequency and duration of moments of self-consciousness depend on the command one has over oneself. So it means that consciousness and will are almost one and the same thing, or, in any case aspects of the same thing.

At this point, it must be understood that the first obstacle in the way of the development of self-consciousness in man, is his conviction that he already possesses self-consciousness or at any rate, that he can have it at any time he likes. It is very difficult to persuade a man that he is not conscious and cannot be conscious at will. It is particularly difficult because here nature plays a very funny trick.

If you ask a man if he is conscious or if you say to him that he is not conscious, he will answer that he is conscious and that it is absurd to say that he is not, because he hears and understands you.

*And he will be quite right, although at the same time quite wrong.* This is nature's trick. He will be right because your question or your remark has made him vaguely conscious for a moment. Next moment consciousness will disappear. But he will remember what you said and what he answered, and he will certainly consider himself conscious.

In reality, acquiring self-consciousness means long and hard work. How can a man agree to this work if he thinks he already possesses the very thing which is promised him as the result of long and hard work? Naturally a man will not begin this work and will not consider it necessary until he becomes convinced that he possesses *neither* self-consciousness *nor* all that is connected with it, that is, unity or individuality, permanent "I" and will.

This brings us to the question of schools, because methods for the development of *self-consciousness, unity, permanent "I" and will*, can be given only by special schools. That must be clearly understood. *Men on the level of relative consciousness cannot find these methods by themselves;* and these methods cannot be described in books or taught in ordinary schools for the very simple reason that they are different for different people, and there is no universal method equally applicable to all.

In other words, this means that men who want to change their state of consciousness need a school. But first, they must realise their need. As long as they think they can do something by themselves they will not be able to make any use of a school, even if they find it. Schools exist only for those who need them, and who know that they need them.

The idea of schools – the study of the kinds of schools that may exist, the study of school principles and school methods – occupies a very important place in the study of that psychology which is connected with the idea of evolution; because without a school there can be no evolution. One cannot even start, because one does not know how to start: still less can one continue or attain anything.

This means that having got rid of the first illusion, that one already has everything one can have, one must get rid of the second illusion that one can get anything by oneself; because by oneself one can get nothing.

These lectures are not a school – not even the beginning of a school. A school requires a much higher pressure of work. But in these lectures I can give to those who wish to listen, some ideas as to how schools work and how they can be found.

I gave before two definitions of psychology.

First, I said that psychology is the study of the possible evolution of man, and second, that psychology is the study of oneself.

I meant that only a psychology which investigates the evolution of man is worth studying, and that a psychology which is occupied with only one phase of man, without knowing anything about his other phases, is obviously not complete, and cannot have any value, even in a purely scientific sense, that is, from the point of view of experiment and observation. For the present phase, as studied by ordinary psychology, in reality does not exist as something separate and consists of many sub-divisions which lead from lower phases to higher phases. Moreover, the same experiment and observation show that one cannot study psychology as one can study any other science not directly connected with oneself. One has to begin the study of psychology with oneself.

Putting together, first what we may know about the next phase in the evolution of man, that is, that it will mean acquiring consciousness, inner unity, permanent ego and will, and second, certain material that we can get by self-observation, that is, realisation of the absence in us of many powers and faculties which we ascribe to ourselves, we come to a new difficulty in understanding the meaning of psychology, and to the necessity for a new definition.

The two definitions given in the previous lectures are not sufficient because man by himself does not know what evolution is possible for him, does not see where he stands at present and ascribes to himself features belonging to higher phases of evolution. In fact, he cannot study himself, being unable to distinguish between the imaginary and the real in himself.

What is lying?

As it is understood in ordinary language, lying means distorting or in some cases, hiding the truth, or what people believe to be the truth. This lying plays a very important part in life, but there are much worse forms of lying, when people do not know that they lie. I said in the last lecture that we cannot know the truth in our present state, and can only know the truth in the state of objective consciousness. How then can we lie? There seems to be a contradiction here, but in reality there is none. We cannot know the truth but we can pretend that we know. *And this is lying.* Lying fills all our life. People pretend that they know all sorts of things: about God, about the future life, about the universe, about the origin of man, about evolution, about everything; but in reality they do not know anything, even about themselves. And every time they speak about something they do not know *as though they knew it, they lie.* Consequently the study of lying becomes of the first importance in psychology.

And it may lead even to the third definition of psychology which is: the study of lying.

Psychology is particularly concerned with the lies a man says and thinks about himself. These lies make the study of man very difficult. Man, as he is, is not a genuine article. He is an imitation of something, and a very bad imitation.

Imagine a scientist on some remote planet who has received from the earth specimens of artificial flowers, *without knowing anything about real flowers.* It will be extremely difficult for him to define them – to explain their shape, their colour, the material from which they are made, that is, wire, cotton-wool and coloured paper – and to classify them in any way.

Psychology stands in a very similar position in relation to man. It has to study an artificial man, without knowing the real man.

Obviously, it cannot be easy to study a being such as man, who does not himself know what is real and what is imaginary in him. So psychology must begin with a division between the real and the imaginary in man.

It is impossible to study man as a whole, because man is divided into two parts: one part which, in some cases, can be almost *all real*, and the other part which, in some cases, can be almost *all imaginary*. In the majority of ordinary men these two parts are intermixed, and cannot be easily distinguished, although they are both there, and both have their own particular meaning and effect.

In the system we are studying, these two parts are called *essence* and *personality*.

Essence is what is *born* in man.

Personality is what is *acquired*. Essence is what is his own. Personality is what is *not* his own. Essence cannot be lost, cannot be changed or injured as easily as personality. Personality can be changed almost completely with the change of circumstances; it can be lost or easily injured.

If I try to describe what essence is, I must, first of all, say that it is the basis of man's physical and mental make-up. For instance, one man is naturally what is called a good sailor, another is a bad sailor, one has a musical ear, another has not, one has a capacity for languages, another has not. This is essence.

Personality is all that is *learned* in one or another way, in ordinary language, "consciously" or "unconsciously." In most cases "unconsciously" means by imitation which, as a matter of fact, plays a very important part in the building of personality. Even in instinctive functions, which naturally should be free from personality, there are usually many so-called "acquired tastes," that is, all sorts of artificial likes and dislikes, all of which are acquired by imitation and imagination. These artificial likes and dislikes play a very important and very disastrous part in man's life. By nature, man should like what is good for him and dislike what is bad for him. But this is so, only as long as essence dominates personality, as it should dominate it, in other words, when a man is healthy and normal. When personality begins to dominate essence and when man becomes less healthy, he begins to like what is bad for him and to dislike what is good for him.

This is connected with the chief thing that can be wrong in the mutual relations of essence and personality.

Normally, essence must dominate personality and then personality can be quite useful. But if personality dominates essence, this produces wrong results of many kinds.

It must be understood that personality is also necessary for man; one cannot live without personality and only with essence. But essence and personality must grow parallel, and the one must not outgrow the other.

Cases of essence outgrowing personality may occur among uneducated people. These so-called simple people may be very good, and even clever, but they are incapable of development in the same way as people with more developed personality.

Cases of personality outgrowing essence are often to be found among more cultured people, and in such cases, essence remains in a half-grown or half-developed state.

This means that with a quick and early growth of personality, growth of essence can practically stop at a very early age, and as a result we see men and women externally quite grown-up, but whose essence remains at the age of ten or twelve.

There are many conditions in modern life which greatly favour this under-development of essence. For instance, the infatuation with sport, *particularly with games*, can very effectively stop the development of essence, and sometimes at such an early age that essence is never fully able to recover later.

This shows that essence cannot be regarded as connected only with the physical constitution, in the simple meaning of the idea. In order to explain more clearly what essence means, I must again return to the study of functions.

I said in the last lecture that the study of man begins with the study of four functions: intellectual, emotional, moving and instinctive. From ordinary psychology, and from ordinary thinking, we know that the intellectual functions, thoughts, and so on, are controlled or produced by a certain *centre* which we call "mind" or "intellect," of "the brain." And this is quite right. Only, to be fully right, we must understand that other functions are also controlled each by its own mind or centre. Thus, from the point of view of the system, there are four minds or centres which control our ordinary actions: intellectual mind, emotional mind, moving mind and instinctive mind. In further references to them we shall call them *centres*. Each centre is quite independent of the others, has its own sphere of action, its own powers, and its own ways of development.

Centres, that is, their structure, capacities, strong sides and defects, belong to essence. Their *contents*, that is, all that a centre acquires, belong to personality. The contents of centres will be explained later.

As I have already said, personality is as equally necessary for the development of man as is essence, only it must stand in its right place. This is hardly possible, because personality is full of wrong ideas about itself. It does not wish to stand in its right place, because its right place is secondary and subordinate; and it does not wish to know the truth about itself, for to know the truth will mean abandoning its falsely dominant position, and occupying the inferior position which rightly belongs to it.

The wrong relative positions of essence and personality determine the present disharmonious state of man. And the only way to get out of this disharmonious state is by self-knowledge.

*To know oneself* – this was the first principle and the first demand of old psychological schools. We still remember these words, but have lost their meaning. We think that *to know ourselves*, means to know our peculiarities, our desires, our tastes, our capacities and our intentions, when in reality it means to know ourselves as machines, that is, to know the *structure* of one's machine, *its parts*, functions of different parts, the conditions governing their work and so on. We realise in a general way that we cannot know any machine without studying it. We must remember this in relation to ourselves and must study our own machines as machines. The means of study is *self-observation.* There is no other way and no one can do this work for us. We must do it ourselves. But before this we must learn *how* to observe. I mean, we must understand the technical side of observation: we must know that it is necessary to observe *different functions* and distinguish between them, remembering, at the same time, about *different states of consciousness*, about our *sleep*, and about the *many* "I"s *in us.*

Such observations will very soon give results. First of all

a man will notice that he cannot observe everything he finds in himself *impartially*. Some things may please him, other things will annoy him, irritate him, even horrify him. And it cannot be otherwise. Man cannot study himself as a remote star, or as a curious fossil. Quite naturally he will like in himself what helps his development and dislike what makes his development more difficult, or even impossible. This means that very soon after starting to observe himself, he will begin to distinguish *useful* features and harmful features in himself, that is, useful or harmful from the point of view of his possible self-knowledge, his possible awakening, his possible development. He will see sides of himself which *can* become conscious, and sides which *cannot* become conscious and *must be eliminated*. In observing himself, he must always remember that his self-study is the first step towards his possible evolution.

Now we must see what are those harmful features that man finds in himself.

Speaking in general they are all mechanical manifestations. The first as has already been said, is *lying*. Lying is unavoidable in mechanical life. No one can escape it and the more one thinks that one is free from lying, the more one is in it. Life, *as it is* could not exist without lying. But from the psychological side, lying has a different meaning. *It means speaking about things one does not know, and even cannot know, as though one knows and can know.*

You must understand that I do not speak from any moral point of view. We have not yet come to questions of what is good, and what is bad, by itself. I speak only from a practical point of view, of what is useful and what is harmful to self-study and self-development.

Starting in this way, man very soon learns to discover signs by which he can know harmful manifestations in himself. He discovers that *the more he can control a manifestation, the less harmful it can be*, and that the less he can control it, that is, the more mechanical it is, the more harmful it can become.

When man understands this he becomes afraid of lying, again not on moral grounds, but on the grounds that he cannot control his lying, and that lying controls him, that is, his other functions.

The second dangerous feature he finds in himself is *imagination*. Very soon after starting his observation of himself he comes to the conclusion that the chief obstacle to observation is imagination. He wishes to observe something, but instead of that, imagination starts in him on the same subject, and he forgets about observation. Very soon he realises that people ascribe to the word imagination a quite artificial and quite undeserved meaning in the sense of *creative or selective faculty*. He realises that imagination is a *destructive faculty*, that he can *never* control it and that it *always* carries him away from his more conscious decisions in a direction in which he had no intention of going. Imagination is almost as bad as lying, it is, in fact, lying to oneself. Man starts to imagine something in order to please himself, and very soon he begins to believe what he imagines, or at least some of it.

Further, or even before that, one finds many very dangerous effects in the *expression of negative emotions*. The term "negative emotions" means all emotions of violence or depression: self-pity, anger, suspicion, fear, annoyance, boredom, mistrust, jealousy and so on. Ordinarily, one accepts this expression of negative emotions as quite natural and even necessary. Very often people call it "sincerity." Of course it has nothing to do with sincerity; it is simply a sign of weakness in man, a sign of bad temper and of incapacity to keep his grievances to himself. Man realises this when he tries to oppose it. And by this he learns another lesson. He realises that in relation to mechanical manifestations it is not enough to observe them, it is necessary to resist them, because without resisting them one cannot observe them. They happen so quickly, so habitually and so imperceptibly, that one cannot notice them if one does not make sufficient efforts to create obstacles for them.

After the *expression of negative emotions* one notices in one self or in other people another curious mechanical feature. This is *talking*. There is no harm in talking by itself. But with some people, especially with those who notice it least, it really becomes a vice. They talk all the time, everywhere they happen to be, while working, while travelling, even while sleeping. They never stop talking to someone if there is someone to talk to, and if there is no one, they talk to themselves.

This too must not only be observed, but resisted as much as possible. With unresisted talking one cannot observe anything, and all the results of a man's observations will immediately evaporate in talking.

The difficulties he has in observing these four manifestations – lying, imagination, the expression of negative emotions and unnecessary talking – will show man his utter mechanicalness, and the impossibility even of struggling against this mechanicalness without help, that is, without new knowledge and without actual assistance. For even if a man has received certain material, he forgets to use it, forgets to observe himself; in other words, he falls asleep again and must always be awakened.

This "falling asleep" has certain definite features of its own, unknown, or at least unregistered and unnamed, in ordinary psychology. These features need special study.

There are two of them. The first is called *identification.*

"Identifying" or "identification" is a curious state in which man passes more than half of his life. He "identifies" with everything: with what he says, what he feels, what he believes, what he does not believe, what he wishes, what he does not wish, what attracts him, what repels him. Everything absorbs him, and he cannot separate himself from the idea, the feeling or the object that absorbed him. This means that in the state of identification man is incapable of looking impartially on the object of his identification. It is difficult to find the smallest thing with which man is unable to "identify." At the same time, in a state of identification, man has even less control over his mechanical reactions than at any other time. Such manifestations as lying, imagination, the expression of negative emotions and constant talking *need identification.* They cannot exist without identification. If man *could* get rid of identification, he could get rid of many useless and foolish manifestations.

Identification, its meaning, causes and results, is extremely well described in the *Philokalia* which was mentioned in the first lecture. But no trace of understanding of it can be found in modem psychology. It is a quite forgotten "psychological discovery."

The second sleep-producing state, akin to identification, is *considering.* Actually, "considering" is identification with people. It is a state in which man constantly worries about what other people think of him; whether they give him his due, whether they admire him enough and so on, and so on. "Considering" plays a very important part in everyone's life, but in some people it becomes an obsession. All their lives are filled with considering, that is, worry, doubt and suspicion, and there remains no place for anything else.

The myth of the "inferiority complex" and other "complexes" is created by the vaguely realised but not understood phenomenon of "identification" and "considering."

Both "identifying" and "considering" must be observed most seriously. Only full knowledge of them can diminish them. If one cannot see them in oneself, one can easily see them in other people. But one must remember that one in no way differs from others. In this sense all people are equal.

Returning now to what was said before, we must try to understand more clearly how the development of man must begin, and in what way self-study can help this beginning.

From the very start we meet with a difficulty in our language. For instance, we want to speak about man from the point of view of evolution. But the word "man" in ordinary language does not admit of any variation or any gradation. Man who is never conscious and never suspects it, man who is struggling to become conscious, man who is fully conscious – it is all the same for our language. It is always "man" in every case. In order to avoid this difficulty and to help the student in classifying his new ideas, the system divides man into *seven categories*.

The first three categories are practically on the same level.

Man No. 1, a man in whom the moving or instinctive

centres predominate over the intellectual and emotional, that is, Physical Man.

Man No. 2, a man in whom the emotional centre predominates over the intellectual, moving and instinctive. Emotional man.

Man No. 3, a man in whom the intellectual centre predominates over the emotional, moving and instinctive. Intellectual man.

In ordinary life we meet only these three categories of man. Each one of us and everyone we know is either No. 1, No. 2, or No. 3. There are higher categories of man, but men are not born already belonging to these higher categories. They are all born No. 1, No. 2, No. 3 and can reach higher categories only through schools.

Man No. 4 is not born as such. He is a product of school culture. He differs from man No. 1, No. 2, and No. 3 by his knowledge of himself, by his understanding of his position and, as it is expressed technically, by his having acquired a permanent centre of gravity. This last means that the idea of acquiring unity, consciousness, permanent "I," and will, that is, the idea of his development has already become for him more important than his other interests.

It must be added to the characteristics of man No. 4, that his functions and centres are more balanced, in a way in which they could not be balanced without work on himself, according to school principles and methods.

Man No. 5 is a man who has acquired *unity* and *self-consciousness*. He is different from ordinary man, because, in him, one of the higher centres already works, and he has many functions and powers that an ordinary man, that is, man No. 1, 2 and 3 does not possess.

Man No. 6 is a man who has acquired *objective*

*consciousness*. Another higher centre works in him. He possesses many more new faculties and powers, beyond the understanding of an ordinary man.

Man No. 7 is a man who has attained all that a man can attain. He has a *permanent "I"* and *free will*. He can control all the states of consciousness in himself and he already cannot lose anything he has acquired. According to another description, *he is immortal within the limits of the solar system.*

Understanding of this division of man into seven categories is very important, for the division has very many applications in all possible ways of studying human activity. It gives, in the hands of those who understand it, a very strong and very fine instrument or tool for the definition of manifestations which, without it, are impossible to define.

Take, for instance, the general concepts of religion, art, science and philosophy. Beginning with religion we can see at once that there must be a religion of man No. 1, that is, all forms of fetishism, no matter how they are called; a religion of man No. 2, that is, emotional, sentimental religion, passing sometimes into fanaticism, the crudest forms of intolerance, persecution of heretics and so on; a religion of man No. 3, that is theoretical, scholastic religion, full of argument about words, forms, rituals, which become more important than anything else; a religion of man No. 4, that is, the religion of man who works for self-development; religion of man No. 5, that is, the religion of a man who has attained unity and can see and know many things that man No. 1, 2, and 3 can neither see nor know; then a religion of man No. 6 and a religion of man No. 7, about neither of which can we know anything.

The same division applies to art, science and philosophy.

There must be an art of man No. 1, an art of man No. 2, an art of man No. 3; science of man No. 1, science of man No. 2, science of man No. 3, science of man No. 4 and so on. You must try to find examples of these for yourselves.

This expansion of concepts greatly enlarges our possibility of finding right solutions to many of our problems.

And this means that the system gives us the possibility of studying *a new language*, that is, new for us, which will connect for us ideas of different categories which are, in reality, united, and divide ideas of seemingly the same categories which are, in reality, different. The division of the word "man" into seven words: Man No. 1, 2, 3, 4, 5, 6, and 7, with all that follows, is an example of this new language.

This gives us the fourth definition of psychology *as the study of a new language.* And this new language is a *universal language*, which people sometimes try to find or invent.

The expression, "a universal language" or "philosophical language," must not be taken in a metaphorical sense. The language is universal in the same sense as mathematical symbols are universal. And besides that it includes in itself all that people can think about. Even the few words of this language which have been explained, give you the possibility of thinking and speaking with more precision than is possible in ordinary language, using any of the existing scientific or philosophical terminologies and nomenclatures.

# THIRD LECTURE

The idea that man is a machine is not a new one. It is really the only scientific view possible; that is, a view based on experiment and observation. A very good definition of man's mechanicalness was given in the so-called "psycho-physiology" of the second part of the nineteenth century. Man was regarded as incapable of any movement without receiving external impressions. Scientists of that time maintained that if it were possible to deprive man, from birth, of all outer and inner impressions and still keep him alive, he would not be able *to make the smallest movement.*

Such an experiment is, of course, impossible even with an animal, because the process of maintaining life, breathing, eating and so on, will produce all sorts of impressions which will start different reflectory movements first, and then awaken the moving centre.

But this idea is interesting because it shows clearly that the activity of the machine depends on external impressions, and begins with responses to these impressions.

Centres in the machine are perfectly adjusted to receive each its own kinds of impressions and to respond to them in a corresponding way. And when centres work rightly, it is possible to calculate the work of the machine and to foresee and foretell many future happenings and responses in the machine, as well as to study them and even direct them.

But unfortunately, centres, even in what is called a healthy and normal man, very rarely work as they should.

The cause of this is that centres are made so that, in a certain way, they can replace one another. In the original plan of Nature the purpose of this was, undoubtedly, to make work of centres continuous and to create a safeguard against possible interruptions in the work of the machine, because in some cases an interruption could be fatal.

But the capacity of centres to work for one another in an untrained and undeveloped machine – as all our machines are – becomes excessive and, as a result, the machine only rarely works with *each centre doing its right work*. Almost every minute one or another centre leaves its own work and tries to do the work of another centre which, in its turn, tries to do the work of a third centre.

I said that centres can replace one another to a certain extent, but not completely, and inevitably in such cases they work in a much less effective way. For instance moving centre can, up to a point, imitate the work of intellectual centre, but it can only produce very vague and disconnected thoughts as, for example, in dreams and in day-dreaming. In its turn, the intellectual centre can work for the moving centre. Try to write, for instance, thinking about every letter you are going to write and how you will write it. You can make experiments of this kind in trying to use your mind to do something which your hands or your legs can do without its help for instance, walk down a staircase noticing every movement, or do some habitual work with your hands, calculating and preparing every small movement by mind. You will immediately see how much more difficult the work will become, how much slower and how much more clumsy the intellectual centre is than the moving centre. You can see this also when you learn some kind of new movement – suppose you learn the use of the typewriter or any kind of new physical work – or take a soldier doing rifle drill. For some time in all your (or his) movements you will depend on the intellectual centre, and only after some time will they begin to pass to moving centre.

Everyone knows the relief when movements become habitual, when the adjustments become automatic, and when there is no need to *think* and calculate every movement all the time. This means that movement has passed to the moving centre, where it normally belongs.

The instinctive centre can work for the emotional, and the emotional can occasionally work for all other centres. And in some cases the intellectual centre has to work for the instinctive centre, although it can only do a very small part of its work, the part which is connected with visible movements, such as the movement of the chest during breathing. It is very dangerous to interfere with normal functions of the instinctive centre, as for instance in artificial breathing, which is sometimes described as yogi breathing, and which must never be undertaken without the advice and observation of a competent and experienced teacher.

Returning to the wrong work of centres, I must say that this fills up practically all our life. Our dull impressions, our vague impressions, our lack of impressions, our slow understanding of many things, very often our identifying and our considering, even our *lying*, all these depend on the wrong work of centres.

The idea of the wrong work of centres does not enter into our ordinary thinking and ordinary knowledge, and we do not realise how much harm it does to us, how much energy we spend unnecessarily in this way and the difficulties into which this wrong work of centres leads us.

Insufficient understanding of the wrong work of our machine is usually connected with the false notion of our unity. When we understand how much divided we are in ourselves, we begin to realise the danger that can lie in the fact that one part of ourselves works instead of another part, without our knowing it.

In the way of self-study and self-observation it is necessary to study and observe not only the right work of centres, but also the wrong work of centres. It is necessary to know all kinds of wrong work and the particular features of the wrong work belonging to particular individuals. It is impossible to know oneself without knowing one's defects and wrong features. And, in addition to general defects belonging to everyone, each of us has his own particular defects belonging only to himself, and they also have to be studied at the right time.

I pointed out in the beginning that the idea that man is a machine brought into motion by external influences is really and truly a scientific idea.

What science does not know is:

*First*, that the human machine does not work up to its standard, and actually works much below its normal standard; that is, not with its full powers, not with all its parts; and

*Second*, that in spite of many obstacles it is capable of developing and creating for itself quite different standards of receptivity and action.

We shall now speak of the conditions necessary for development because it must be remembered that although development is possible, it is at the same time very rare and requires a great number of external and internal conditions.

What are these conditions?

The first of these conditions is that man must understand his position, his difficulties and his possibilities and must have either a very strong desire to get out of his present state or have a very great interest *for the new, for the unknown state which must come with the change.* Speaking shortly, he must be either very strongly repelled by his present state or very strongly attracted by the future state that may be attained.

Further, one must have a certain preparation. A man must be able to understand what he is told.

Also, he must be in right conditions externally, he must have sufficient free time for study and must live in circumstances which make study possible.

It is impossible to enumerate all the conditions which are necessary. But they include among other things a school. And school implies such social and political conditions in the given country in which a school can exist, because a school cannot exist in any conditions; and a more or less ordered life and a certain level of culture and *personal freedom* are necessary for the existence of a school. Our time is particularly difficult in this respect. Schools in the East are disappearing very quickly. In many countries they are absolutely impossible. For instance, no school could exist in Bolshevik Russia, or in Hitler's Germany, or in Mussolini's Italy, or in Kemal's Turkey.

I quoted some verses from the *Laws of Manu* referring to this subject in the *New Model of the Universe*.

From the rules for a Snataka (householder):

61. He must not live in a country governed by Sudras, nor in one inhabited by impious men, nor in one conquered by heretics, nor one abounding with men of lower castes.

79. He must not be in the company of outcastes, nor of *Kandalas*, the lowest of men, nor of *Pukkases*, nor of idiots, nor of arrogant men, nor of men of low class, nor of *Antyavasayins* (grave-diggers).

*Chapter VIII.*

22. A kingdom peopled mostly by Sudras filled with godless men and deprived of twice-born inhabitants, will soon wholly perish, stricken by hunger and disease.

These ideas of the *Laws of Manu* are very interesting because they give us a basis on which we can judge different political and social conditions *from the point of view of school-work*, and to see which conditions are really progressive, and which bring only the destruction of all real values, although their adherents pretend that these conditions are progressive and even manage to deceive quantities of weak-minded people.

But external conditions do not depend on us. To a certain extent, and sometimes with great difficulty, we can choose the country where we prefer to live, but we cannot choose the period of the century and must try to find what we want in the period in which we are placed by fate.

So we must understand that even the beginning of preparation for development needs a combination of external and internal conditions which only rarely come all together.

But at the same time, we must understand that at least so far as internal conditions are concerned, man is not entirely left to the law of accident. There are many lights arranged for him by which he can find his way if he cares to and if he is *lucky*. His possibility is so small that the element of *luck* cannot be excluded.

Let us now try to answer the question: What makes a man desire to acquire new knowledge and to change himself?

Man lives in life under *two kinds of influences*. This must be very well understood and the difference between the two kinds of influences must be very clear.

The first kind consists of interests and attractions created *by life itself*: interests of one's health, safety, wealth, pleasures, amusements, security, vanity, pride, fame, etc.

The second kind consists of interests of a different order aroused by ideas which are not created in life but *come originally from schools*. These influences do not reach man directly. They are thrown into the general turnover of life, pass through many different minds and reach a man through philosophy, science, religion and art, always mixed with influences of the first kind and generally very little resembling what they were in their beginning.

In most cases men do not realise the different origin of the influences of the second kind and often explain them as having the same origin as the first kind.

Although man does not know of the existence of two kinds of influences, they both act on him and in one way or another way he responds to them.

He can be more identified with one or with some of the influences of the first kind and not feel influences of the second kind at all. Or he can be attracted and affected by one or another of the influences of the second kind. The result is different in each case.

We will call the first kind of influence, influence *A* and the second, influence *B*.

If a man is fully in the power of influence A, or of one particular influence A, and quite indifferent to influence B, nothing happens to him and his possibility of development diminishes with every year of his life, and at a certain age, sometimes quite an early age, it disappears completely. This means that man dies while physically remaining still alive, like grain that cannot germinate and produce a plant.

But if, on the other hand, man is not completely in the

power of influence A and if influences B attract him and make him feel and think, *results of the impressions they produce collect in him together,* attract other influences of the same kind and grow, occupying a more important place in his mind and life.

If the results produced by influence B become sufficiently strong, they fuse together and form in man what is called a *magnetic centre*. It must be understood at once that the word "centre" in this case does not mean the same thing as the "intellectual" or the "moving" centre; that is, centres in the essence. The *Magnetic centre* is in personality, it is simply a group of interests which, when they become sufficiently strong, serve, to a certain degree, as a guiding and controlling factor. Magnetic centre turns one's interests in a certain direction and helps to keep them there. At the same time it cannot do much by itself. A school is necessary. Magnetic centre cannot replace a school, but it can help to realise the need of a school; it can help to begin to look for a school, or if one meets a school by chance, magnetic centre can help to recognise a school and try not to lose it. Because nothing is easier to lose than a school.

Possession of a magnetic centre is the first, although quite unspoken, demand of a school. If a man without a magnetic centre, or a small or a weak magnetic centre, or with several contradictory magnetic centres, that is, interested in many incompatible things at the same time, meets a school, he does not become interested in it, or he becomes critical at once before he can know anything, or his interest disappears very quickly when he meets with the first difficulties of school work. This is the chief safeguard of a school. Without it the school would be filled with quite a wrong kind of people who would immediately distort the school teaching. A right magnetic centre not only helps one to recognise a school, it also helps to absorb the school teaching which is different from both influences A and influences B and may be called influence C.

Influence C can be transferred only by word of mouth, by direct instruction, explanation and demonstration.

When a man meets with influence C and is able to absorb it, it is said about him that in one point of himself; that is, in *magnetic centre,* he becomes free from the law of accident. From this moment the magnetic centre has actually played its part. It brought man to a school or helped him in his first steps there. From then on the ideas and the teaching of the school take the place of magnetic centre and slowly begin to penetrate into the different parts of personality and with time into essence.

One can learn many things about schools, about their organisation and about their activity in the ordinary way by reading and by studying historical periods when schools were more conspicuous and more accessible. But there are certain things about schools that one can learn only in schools themselves. And the explanation of school principles and rules occupies a very considerable place in school teaching.

One of the most important principles one learns in this way is that real school work must proceed *by three lines* simultaneously. One line of work, or two lines of work, cannot be called real "school work."

What are these three lines?

In the first lecture I said that these lectures are not a school. Now I will be able to explain why they are not a school.

Once at a lecture a question was asked: Do people who study this system work only for themselves or do they work for other people? Now I will also answer this question.

The first line is study of oneself and study of the system, or the "language." Working on this line one certainly works *for oneself.*

The second line is work with other people in the school and working with them, one works not only with them *but for* them. So in the second line one learns to work with people and for people.

This is why the second line is particularly difficult for some people.

In the third line, one works *for the school.* In order to work for the school, one must first *understand* the work of the school, understand its aims and needs. And this requires time unless one is really well prepared, because some people can *begin* with the third line, or in any case find it very easily.

When I said that these lectures are not a school, I meant that these lectures give the possibility of only one line of work; that is, study of the system and self-study. It is true that even by learning together people study the beginning of the second line of work, at least they learn to *bear one another*, and if their thought is broad enough and their perception quick enough they can even grasp something about the second and third lines of work. Still one cannot expect much just from lectures.

In the second line of work, in complete school organisation, people must not only *talk* together, but *work* together, and this work can be very different but must always, in one or another way, *be useful to the school.* So it means that working in the first line people study the second line and working in the second line they study the third line. Later you will learn why three lines are necessary and why only three lines of work can proceed successfully and towards a definite aim.

Even now you can understand the chief reason of the necessity of three lines of work if you realise that man is asleep and whatever work he starts, he soon loses interest in it and continues mechanically. Three lines of work are necessary, first of all, because one line awakes a man who falls asleep over another line. If one really works on three lines, one can never fall asleep completely; in any case one cannot sleep as happily as before; one will always awake and realise that one's work has stopped.

I can show also one very characteristic difference between three lines of work.

In the first line, one works chiefly on the study of the system or self-study and on self-observation, and one must manifest in one's work a certain amount of initiative in relation to oneself.

In the second line one works in connection with certain organised work and one must only *do what one is told*. No initiative is required or admitted in the second line and the chief point in this is *discipline* and following exactly what one is told, without bringing in any of one's own ideas even if they appear better than those that have been given.

In the third line again one can manifest more initiative, but one must always *verify* oneself and not let oneself make decisions against rules and principles, or against what one has been told.

I said before that the work begins with the study of the language. It will be very useful if at this point you try to realise that you already know a certain number of words of this new language, and it will also be very useful if you try to count these new words and write them down together. Only they must be written down without any comments; that is, without interpretation – comments and interpretations or explanations must be in your understanding. You cannot put them on paper. If this were possible, the study of psychological teachings would be very simple. It would be sufficient to publish a sort of dictionary or glossary and people would know all that it is necessary to know. But, fortunately or unfortunately, this is impossible and men have to learn and work each for himself.

We must again return to centres and find why we cannot develop more quickly without the necessity for long school work.

We know that when we learn something, we accumulate new material in our memory. But what is our memory? In order to understand this, we must learn to regard each centre as a separate and independent machine, consisting of a sensitive matter similar to *the mass of phonographic rolls*. All that happens to us, all that we see, all that we hear, all that we feel, all that we learn is registered on these rolls. It means that all external and internal events leave certain "impressions" on the rolls. "Impressions" is a very good word because it actually is *an impression* or an *imprint*. An impression can be deep, or it can be very slight, or it can be simply a glancing impression that disappears very quickly and leaves no trace after it. But whether deep or slight they are impressions. And these impressions on rolls are all that we have, all our possessions. Everything that we know, everything that we have learned, everything that we have experienced is all there on our rolls. Exactly in the same way all our thought processes, calculations, speculations consist only of comparing the inscriptions on rolls, reading them again and again, trying to understand them by putting them together, and so on. We can think of nothing new, nothing that is not on our rolls. We can neither say nor do anything that does not correspond to some inscription on the rolls. We cannot invent a new thought in the same way as we cannot invent a new animal, because all our ideas of animals are created by our observation of existing animals.

Inscriptions or impressions on rolls are connected by associations. Associations connect impressions either received simultaneously or in some way similar to one another.

In my first lecture I said that memory depends on consciousness and that we actually remember only the moments when we had flashes of consciousness. It is quite clear that different simultaneous impressions connected together will remain longer in memory than unconnected impressions. In the flash of self-consciousness, or even near it, all impressions of the moment are connected and remain connected in the memory. The same refers to impressions connected by their inner similarity. If one is more conscious in the moment of receiving impressions, one connects more definitely the new impressions with similar old impressions and they remain connected in memory. On the other hand if one receives impressions in a state of identification, one simply does not notice them and their traces disappear before they can be appreciated or associated. In the state of identification one does not see and one does not hear. One is wholly in one's grievance, or in one's desire, or in one's imagination. One cannot separate oneself from things or feelings or memories and one is shut off from all the world around.

## FOURTH LECTURE

We shall begin today with a more detailed examination of centres. This is the diagram of the four centres:

| | |
|---|---|
| Intellectual centre | Head |
| Emotional centre | Middle part of the body<br>Chest |
| Moving centre<br>Instinctive centre | Lower part of the body<br>and back |

The diagram represents a man standing sideways, looking to the left, and indicates the relative position of centres in a very schematic way.

*In reality each centre occupies the whole body*, penetrates, so to speak, the whole organism. At the same time, each centre has what is called its "centre of gravity." The centre of gravity of the intellectual centre is in the brain; the centre of gravity of the emotional centre is in the solar plexus; the centres of gravity of the moving and instinctive centres are in the spinal cord.

It must be understood that in the present state of scientific knowledge we have no means of verifying this statement, chiefly because each centre includes in itself many properties which are still unknown to ordinary science and *even to anatomy*. It may sound strange, but the fact is that the anatomy of the human body is far from being a completed science.

So the study of centres, which are hidden from us, must begin with the observation of their functions, which are quite open for our investigation.

This is quite a usual course. In the different sciences – physics, chemistry, astronomy, physiology – when we cannot reach the facts or objects or matters we wish to study, we have to begin with an investigation of their *results* or *traces*. In this case we shall be dealing with the direct functions of centres; so all that we establish about functions can be applied to centres.

All centres have much in common and, at the same time, each centre has its own peculiar characteristics which must always be kept in mind.

One of the most important principles that must be understood in relation to centres is the great difference in their speed, that is, a difference in the speeds of their functions.

*The slowest is the intellectual centre*. Next to it – although very much faster – stand the moving and instinctive centres, which have more or less the same speed. The fastest of all is the emotional centre, though in the state of "waking sleep" it works only very rarely with anything approximating to its real speed, and generally works with the speed of the instinctive and moving centres.

Observations can help us to establish a great difference in the speeds of functions, but they cannot give us the exact figures. In reality the difference is very great, greater than one can imagine as being possible between functions of the same organism. As I have just said, with our ordinary means we cannot calculate the difference in the speed of centres, but, if we are told what it is, we can find many facts which will confirm not the figures but the existence of the enormous difference.

So before bringing in figures, I want to speak about ordinary observations which can be made without any special knowledge.

Try, for instance, to compare the speed of mental processes with moving functions. Try to observe yourself when you have to perform many quick simultaneous movements, as when driving a car in a very crowded street, or riding fast on a bad road, or doing any work requiring quick judgment and quick movements. You will see at once that you cannot observe all your movements. You will either have to slow them down or miss the greater part of your observations; otherwise you will risk an accident and probably have one if you persist in observing. There are many similar observations which can be made, particularly on the emotional centre which is still faster. Everyone of us really has many observations on the different speeds of our functions, but only very rarely do we know the value of our observations and experiences. Only when we know the principle do we begin to understand our own previous observations.

At the same time it must be said that all the figures referring to these different speeds are established and known in school systems. As you will see later, the difference in the speed of centres is a very strange figure which has a cosmic meaning, that is, it enters into many cosmic processes or, it is better to say it divides many cosmic processes one from another. This figure is 30,000. This means that the moving and instinctive centres are 30,000 times faster than the intellectual centre. And the emotional centre 30,000 times faster than the moving and instinctive centres.

It is difficult to believe in such an enormous difference in the speeds of functions in the same organism. It actually means that different centres have a quite *different* time. The instinctive and moving centres have 30,000 times longer time than the intellectual centre, and the emotional centre has 30,000 times longer time than the moving and instinctive centres.

Do you understand clearly what "longer time" means? It means that, for every kind of work that a centre has to do, it has so much more time. However strange it may be, this fact of the great difference in the speed of centres explains many well-known phenomena which ordinary science cannot explain and which it generally passes over in silence, or simply refuses to discuss. I am referring now to the astonishing and quite inexplicable speed of some of the physiological and mental processes.

For instance – a man drinks a glass of brandy, and *immediately* in no more than a second, he experiences many new feelings and sensations – a feeling of warmth, relaxation, relief, peace, contentment, well-being, or on the other hand, anger, irritation, and so on. What he feels may be different in different cases, but the fact remains that the body responds to the stimulant *very quickly*, almost at once.

There is really no need to speak about brandy or any other stimulant; if a man is very thirsty or very hungry, a glass of water or a piece of bread will produce the same quick effect.

Similar phenomena representing the enormous speed of certain processes can be noticed, for instance, in observing dreams, I referred to some of these observations in *A New Model of the Universe*.

The difference is again either between the instinctive and the intellectual centres or between the moving and the intellectual. But we are so accustomed to these phenomena that we rarely think how strange and incomprehensible they are.

Of course, for a man who has never thought about himself and never tried to study himself, there is nothing strange in this or in anything else. But in reality, from the point of view of ordinary physiology, these phenomena look almost miraculous.

A physiologist knows how many complicated processes must be gone through between swallowing brandy or a glass of water and feeling its effects. Every substance entering the body by way of the mouth has to be analysed, tried in several different ways and only then accepted or rejected. And all this happens in one second or less. It is a miracle, and at the same time it is not. For, if we know the difference in the speed of centres and remember that the instinctive centre, which has to do this work, has 30,000 times more time than the intellectual centre by which we measure our ordinary time, we can understand how it may happen. It means that the instinctive centre has not one second, but *about eight hours* of its own time for this work, and in eight hours this work can certainly be done in an ordinary laboratory without any unnecessary haste. So our idea of the extraordinary speed of this work is purely an illusion which we have because we think that our ordinary time, or the time of the intellectual centre, is the only time which exists.

We shall return later on to the study of the difference in speed of centres.

Now we must try to understand another characteristic of centres which will later give us very good material for self-observation and for work upon ourselves.

It is supposed that each centre is divided into two parts, positive and negative.

This division is particularly clear in the intellectual centre and in the instinctive centre.

All the work of the intellectual centre is divided into two parts: *affirmation* and *negation*; *yes* and *no*. In every moment of our thinking, either one outweighs the other or they come to a moment of equal strength in indecision. The negative part of the intellectual centre is as useful as the positive part, and any diminishing of the strength of the one in relation to the other results in mental disorders.

In the work of the instinctive centre the division is also quite clear, and both parts, positive and negative, or pleasant and unpleasant, are equally necessary for a right orientation in life.

Pleasant sensations of taste, smell, touch, temperature, warmth, coolness, fresh air – all indicate conditions which are beneficial for life; and unpleasant sensations of bad taste, bad smell, unpleasant touch, feeling of oppressive heat or extreme cold, all indicate conditions which can be harmful to life.

It may definitely be said that no true orientation in life is possible without both pleasant and unpleasant sensations. They are the real guidance of all animal life on the earth and any defect in them results in a lack of orientation and a consequent danger of illness and death. Think how quickly a man would poison himself if he lost all sense of taste and smell, or if, in some unnatural way, he conquered in himself a natural disgust of unpleasant sensations.

In the moving centre the division into two parts, positive and negative, has only a logical meaning; that is, movement as opposed to rest. It has no meaning for practical observation.

In the emotional centre, at a first glance, the division is quite simple and obvious. If we take pleasant emotions such as joy, sympathy, affection, self-confidence, as belonging to the positive part, and unpleasant emotions such as boredom, irritation, jealousy, envy, fear, as belonging to the negative part, things will look very simple; but in reality they are much more complicated.

To begin with, in the emotional centre there is no natural negative part. The greater part of negative emotions are artificial; they do not belong to the emotional centre proper and are based on instinctive emotions which are quite unrelated to them but which are transformed by imagination and identification. This is the real meaning of the theory of James and Lange, at one time very well-known. They insisted that all emotions were really sensations of changes in inner organs and tissues, changes which took place before sensations, and were the actual cause of sensations. That really meant that external events and inner realisations did not produce emotions. External events and inner realisations produced inner reflexes which produced sensations; and these were interpreted as emotions. At the same time positive emotions such as "love," "hope," "faith," in the sense in which they are usually understood – that is, as permanent emotions – are impossible for a man in the *ordinary* state of consciousness. They require higher states of consciousness; they require inner unity, self-consciousness, permanent "I" and will.

*Positive emotions are emotions which cannot become negative.* But all our pleasant emotions such as joy, sympathy, affection, self-confidence, can, at any moment, turn into boredom, irritation envy, fear and so on. Love can turn into jealousy or fear to lose what one loves, or into anger and hatred; hope can turn into day-dreaming and the expectation of impossible things, and faith can turn into superstition and a weak acceptance of comforting nonsense.

Even a purely intellectual emotion – the desire for knowledge, or an aesthetic emotion; that is, a feeling of beauty or harmony – if it becomes mixed with identification, immediately unites with emotions of a negative kind such as self-pride, vanity, selfishness, conceit and so on.

So we can say without any possibility of mistake that we can have no positive emotions. At the same time, in actual fact, we have no negative emotions which exist without imagination and identification. Of course it cannot be denied that besides the many and varied kinds of physical suffering which belong to the instinctive centre, man has many kinds of mental suffering which belong to the emotional centre. He has many sorrows, griefs, fears, apprehensions and so on which cannot be avoided and are as closely connected with man's life as illness, pain and death. But these mental sufferings are very different from negative emotions which are based on imagination and identification.

These emotions are a terrible phenomenon. They occupy an enormous place in our life. Of many people it is possible to say that all their lives are regulated and controlled, and in the end ruined, *by negative emotions*. At the same time negative emotions do not play any useful part at all in our lives. They do not help our orientation, they do not give us any knowledge, they do not guide us in any sensible manner. On the contrary, they spoil all our pleasures, they make life a burden to us and they very effectively prevent our possible development *because there is nothing more mechanical in our life than negative emotions.*

Negative emotions can never come under our control. People who think they can control their negative emotions and manifest them when they want to, simply deceive themselves. Negative emotions depend on identification; if identification is destroyed in some particular case, they disappear. The strangest and most fantastic fact about negative emotions is that people actually worship them. I think that, for an ordinary mechanical man, the most difficult thing to realise is that his own and other people's negative emotions, have no value whatever and *do not contain anything noble, anything beautiful or anything strong.* In reality negative emotions contain nothing but weakness and very often the beginning of hysteria, insanity or crime. The only good thing about them is that, being quite useless and artificially created by imagination and identification, they can be destroyed without any loss. And this is the only chance of escape that man has.

If negative emotions were useful or necessary for any, even the smallest purpose, and if they were a function of a really existing part of the emotional centre, man would have no chance because no inner development is possible so long as man keeps his negative emotions.

In school language it is said on the subject of the struggle with negative emotions:

*Man must sacrifice his suffering.*

"What could be easier to sacrifice?" everyone will say. But in reality people would sacrifice anything rather than their negative emotions. There is no pleasure and no enjoyment man would not sacrifice for quite small reasons, but he will never sacrifice his suffering. And in a sense there is a reason for this.

In a quite superstitious way man expects to gain something by sacrificing his pleasures, but he cannot expect anything for sacrifice of his suffering. He is full of wrong ideas about suffering – he still thinks that suffering is sent to him by God or by gods for his punishment or for his edification, and he will even be afraid to hear of the possibility of getting rid of his suffering in such a simple way. The idea is made even more difficult by the existence of many sufferings from which man really cannot get rid, and of many other sufferings which are entirely based on man's imagination, which he cannot and will not give up, like the idea of injustice, for instance, and the belief in the possibility of destroying injustice.

Besides that many people have nothing but negative emotions. All their "I"s are negative. If you were to take negative emotions away from them, they would simply collapse and go up in smoke.

And what would happen to all our life, without negative emotions? What would happen to what we call art, to the theatre, to drama, to most novels?

Unfortunately there is no chance of negative emotions disappearing. Negative emotions can be conquered and can disappear only with the help of school knowledge and school methods. The struggle against negative emotions is a part of school training and is closely connected with all school work.

What is the origin of negative emotions if they are artificial, unnatural and useless? As we do not know the origin of man we cannot discuss this question, and we can speak about negative emotions and their origin only in relation to ourselves and our lives. For instance, in watching children we can see how they are *taught negative emotions* and how they learn them themselves through imitation of grown-ups and older children.

If, from the earliest days of his life, a child could be put among people who have no negative emotions, he would probably have none, or so very few that they could be easily conquered by right education. But in actual life things happen quite differently, and with the help of all the examples he can see and hear, with the help of reading, the cinema and so on, a child of about ten already knows the whole scale of negative emotions and can imagine them, reproduce them, and identify with them as well as any grown-up man.

In grown-up people negative emotions are supported by the constant justification and glorification of them in literature and art, and by personal self-justification and self-indulgence. Even when we become tired of them we do not believe that we can become quite free from them.

In reality, we have much more power over negative emotions than we think, particularly when we already know how dangerous they are and how urgent is the struggle with them. But we find too many excuses for them, and swim in the seas of self-pity and selfishness, as the case may be, finding fault in everything except ourselves.

All that has just been said shows that we are in a very strange position in relation to our emotional centre. It has no positive part, and no negative part. Most of its negative functions are invented and there are many people who have never in their lives experienced any *real* emotion, so completely is their time occupied with imaginary emotions.

So we cannot say that our emotional centre is divided

into two parts, positive and negative. We can only say that we have *pleasant* emotions and *unpleasant* emotions, and that all of them which are not negative at a given moment *can turn into negative emotions under the slightest provocations or even without any provocation.*

This is the true picture of our emotional life and if we look sincerely at ourselves we must realise that so long as we cultivate and admire in ourselves all these poisonous emotions we cannot expect to be able to develop *unity, consciousness* or *will.* If such development were possible, then all these negative emotions would enter into our new being and become permanent in us. This would mean that it would be impossible for us ever to get rid of them. Luckily for us, such a thing cannot happen.

In our present state the only good thing about us is that there is nothing permanent in us. If anything becomes permanent in our present state, it means insanity. Only lunatics can have a permanent ego.

Incidentally this fact disposes of another false term that crept into the psychological language of the day from the so-called psychoanalysis: I mean the word "complex."

There is nothing in our psychological make-up that corresponds to the idea of "complex." In the psychiatry of the nineteenth century, what is now called "complex" was called a "*fixed* idea," and "fixed ideas" were taken as signs of insanity. And that remains perfectly correct.

Normal man cannot have "fixed ideas" "complexes" or "fixations." It is useful to remember this in case someone tries to find complexes in you. We have many bad features as it is and our chances are very small even without complexes.

Returning now to the question of work on ourselves

we must ask ourselves what our chances actually are. We must discover in ourselves functions and manifestations which we can, to a certain extent, control, and we must exercise control, trying to increase it as much as possible. For instance, we have a certain control over our movements, and in many schools, particularly in the East, work on oneself begins with acquiring as full a control over movements as possible. But this needs special training, very much time and the study of very elaborate exercises. Under the conditions of modern life we have more control over our thoughts, and in connection with this there is a special method by which we may work on the development of our consciousness using that instrument which is most obedient to our will; that is, our mind, or the intellectual centre.

In order to understand more clearly what I am going to say, you must try to remember that we have no control over our consciousness. When I said that we can become more conscious, or that a man can be made conscious for a moment simply by asking him if he is conscious or not, I used the words "conscious" or "consciousness" in a relative sense. There are so many degrees of consciousness and every higher degree means "consciousness" in relation to a lower degree. But, if we have no control over consciousness itself, we have a certain control over our thinking about consciousness, and we can construct our thinking in such a way as to bring consciousness. What I mean is that by giving to our thoughts the direction which they would have in a moment of consciousness, we can, in this way, induce consciousness.

Now try to formulate what you noticed when you tried to observe yourself.

You noticed three things. First, that you do not *remember yourself*; that is, that you are not aware of yourself at the time when you try to observe yourself. Second, that observation is made difficult by the incessant stream of thoughts, images, echoes of conversation, fragments of emotions, flowing through your mind and very often distracting your attention from observation. And third, that the moment you start self-observation something in you starts imagination, and self-observation, if you really try it, is a constant struggle with imagination.

Now this is the chief point in work upon oneself. If one realises that all the difficulties in the work depend on the fact that one cannot *remember oneself*, one already knows what one must do.

*One must try to remember oneself.*

In order to do this one must struggle with mechanical thoughts and one must struggle with imagination.

If one does this conscientiously and persistently one will see results in a comparatively short time. But one must not think that it is easy or that one can master this practice immediately.

*Self-remembering*, as it is called, is a very difficult thing to learn to practice. It must not be based on an expectation of results, otherwise one can identify with one's efforts. It must be based on the realisation of the fact that we do not remember ourselves, and that at the same time we *can* remember ourselves, if we try sufficiently hard and in the right way.

We cannot become conscious at will, at the moment when we want to, because we have no command over states of consciousness. But we can *remember ourselves* for a short time at will, because we have a certain command over our thoughts. And if we start remembering ourselves, by the special construction of our thoughts – that is, by the realisation that we do not remember ourselves, that nobody remembers himself, and by realising all that this means – this will bring us to consciousness.

You must remember that we have found the weak spot in the walls of our mechanicalness. This is the knowledge that we do not remember ourselves; and the realisation that we can try to remember ourselves. Up to this moment our task has only been self-study. Now, with the understanding of the necessity for actual change in ourselves, work begins.

Later on you will learn that the practice of self-remembering, connected with self-observation and with the struggle against imagination, has not only a psychological meaning, but it also changes the subtlest part of our metabolism and produces definite chemical, or perhaps it is better to say alchemical, effects in our body. So today from psychology we have come to alchemy; that is, to the idea of the transformation of coarse elements into finer ones.

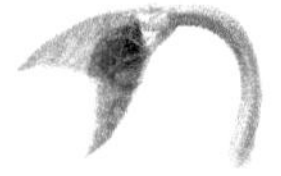

# FIFTH LECTURE

In relation to the study of man's possible development I must establish one very important point.

There are two sides of man that must be developed, that is, there are two lines of possible development that must proceed simultaneously.

These two sides of man, or two lines of possible development, are *knowledge* and *being*.

I have already spoken many times about the necessity for the development of knowledge, and particularly self-knowledge, because one of the most characteristic features of man's present state is that *he does not know himself.*

Generally people understand the idea of different levels of knowledge, the idea of the relativity of knowledge and the necessity for quite new knowledge.

What people do not understand in most cases is the idea of *being* as quite separate from knowledge; and further, the idea of the relativity of being, the possibility of different levels of being and the necessity for the development of being, separately from the development of knowledge.

A Russian philosopher, Vladimir Solovieff, used the term "being" in his writings. He spoke about the being of a stone, the being of a plant, the being of an animal, the being of a man and the divine being.

This is better than the ordinary concept because in ordinary understanding the being of a man is not regarded as in any way different from the being of a stone, the being of a plant or the being of an animal. From the ordinary point of view a stone, a plant, an animal *are* or *exist* exactly as a man *is* or *exists*. In reality, they exist quite differently. But Solovieff's division is not sufficient. There is no such thing as *the being of a man*. Men are too different for that. I have already explained that, from the point of view of the system we are studying, the concept of man is divided into seven concepts: man No. 1, man No. 2, man No. 3, man No. 4, man No. 5, man No. 6, and man No. 7. This means seven degrees or categories of being: being No. 1, being No. 2, being No. 3 and so on. In addition to this we already know finer divisions. We know that there may be very different men No. 1, very different men No. 2, and very different men No. 3. They may live entirely under influences A. They may be equally affected by influences A and B. They may be more under influences B than A. They may have a magnetic centre. They may have come into contact with school influence or influence C. They may be on the way to becoming men No. 4. All these categories indicate different levels of being.

The idea of being entered into the very foundation of thinking and speaking about man in religious thought, and all other divisions of man were regarded as unimportant in comparison with this. Men were divided into pagans, unbelievers or heretics on the one hand, and into true believers, righteous men, saints, prophets and so on. All these definitions referred not to differences in views and convictions, that is, *not to knowledge*, but to *being*.

In modern thought people ignore the idea of being and different levels of being. On the contrary, they believe that the more discrepancies and contradictions there are in a man's being, the more interesting and brilliant he can be. It is generally, although tacitly, and not always even tacitly, admitted that a man can be given to lying, he can be selfish, unreliable, unreasonable, perverted, and yet be a great scientist or a great philosopher or a great artist. Of course this is quite impossible. This incompatibility of different features of one's being, which is generally regarded as originality, actually means weakness. One cannot be a great thinker or a great artist with a perverted or an inconsistent mind, just as one cannot be a prizefighter or a circus athlete with consumption. The widespread acceptance of the idea that inconsistency and amorality means originality is responsible for the many scientific, artistic and religious fakes of our present time and probably of all times.

It is necessary to understand clearly what *being* means, and why it must grow and develop side by side with knowledge, but independently of it.

If knowledge outgrows being or being outgrows knowledge, the result is always a one-sided development, and a one-sided development cannot go far. It is bound to come to some inner contradiction of a serious nature and stop there.

Some time later we may speak about the different kinds and the different results of one-sided development. Ordinarily, in life we meet with only one kind, that is, when knowledge has outgrown being. The result takes the form of a dogmatization of certain ideas and the consequent impossibility of a further development of knowledge because of the loss of understanding.

Now I shall speak about understanding.

What is understanding?

Try to ask yourself this question and you will see that you cannot answer it. You have always confused *understanding* with *knowing* or having information. But to know and to understand are two quite different things and you must learn to distinguish between them.

In order to understand a thing, you must see its connection with some bigger subject, or bigger whole, and the possible consequences of this connection. Understanding is always the understanding of a smaller problem in relation to a bigger problem.

For instance, suppose I show you an old Russian silver rouble. It was a piece of money the size of a halfcrown and corresponding to two shillings and a penny. You may look at it, study it, notice in which year it was coined, find out everything about the Tsar whose portrait is on one side, weigh it, even make a chemical analysis and determine the exact quantity of silver contained in it. You can learn what the word "rouble" means and how it came into use. You can learn all these things and probably many more, but you will not *understand it and its meaning* if you do not find out that before the last war its purchasing power corresponded in many cases to a present-day English pound, and that the present-day paper rouble in Bolshevik Russia corresponds in many cases to an English farthing or even less. If you find out this you will *understand* something about a rouble and perhaps also about some other things, because the understanding of one thing immediately leads to the understanding of many other things.

Often people even think understanding means finding a name, a word, a title or a label for a new or unexpected phenomenon. This finding or inventing of words for incomprehensible things has nothing to do with understanding. On the contrary, if we could get rid of half of our words perhaps we should have a better chance of a certain understanding.

If we ask ourselves what it means to understand or not to understand a man, we must first think of an instance of not being able to speak with a man in his own language. Naturally two people having no common language will not understand one another. They must have a common language or agree on certain signs or symbols by which they will designate things. But suppose that during a conversation with a man you disagree about the meaning of certain words or signs or symbols, then you again cease to understand one another.

From this follows the principle that you *cannot understand and disagree*. In ordinary conversation we very often say: I understand him but I do not agree with him. From the point of view of the system we are studying, this is impossible. If you understand a man, you agree with him; if you disagree with him, you do not understand him.

It is difficult to accept this idea and this means that it is difficult to understand it.

As I have just said, there are two sides of man which must develop in the normal course of his evolution: knowledge and being. But neither knowledge nor being can stay still or remain in the same state. If either of them does not grow bigger and stronger, it becomes smaller and weaker.

Understanding may be compared to an *arithmetical mean* between knowledge and being. It shows the necessity for a simultaneous growth of knowledge and being. The growth of only one and diminishing of another will not change the arithmetical mean.

This also explains why "to understand" means to agree. People who understand one another must not only have an equal knowledge, they must also have an equal being. Only then is mutual understanding possible.

Another wrong idea which people have or which belongs particularly to our times, is that understanding can be different, that people *can* – that is, have the right – to understand the same thing differently.

This is quite wrong from the point of view of the system. Understanding cannot be different. There can only be one *understanding*, the rest is non-understanding, or incomplete understanding.

But at the same time people often think that they understand things differently. We can see examples of this every day. How can we find an explanation of this seeming contradiction?

In reality, there is no contradiction. Understanding means understanding of a part in relation to the whole. But the idea of the whole can be very different in people according to their knowledge and being. This is why the system is again necessary. People learn to understand by understanding the system and everything else in relation to the system.

But speaking on an ordinary level without the idea of a school or a system, one must admit that there are as many understandings as there are many people. Everyone understands everything in his own way or according to one or another mechanical training or habit; but this is all a subjective and relative understanding. The way to objective understanding lies through school systems and the change of being.

In order to explain this I must return to the division of man into seven categories.

You must realise that there is a great difference between men No. 1, 2 and 3 on one hand and men of higher categories on another hand. In reality the difference is much greater than we can imagine. It is so great that all life from this point of view is regarded as being divided into two concentric circles – the inner circle and the outer circle of humanity.

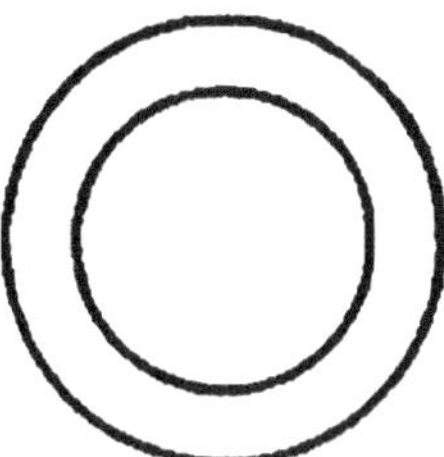

To the inner circle belong men No. 5, 6 and 7; to the outer circle, men No. 1, 2 and 3. Men No. 4 are on the threshold of the inner circle or between the two circles.

The inner circle is in its turn divided into three concentric circles; the innermost, to which belong men No. 7, the middle to which belong men No. 6, and the outer-inner circle to which belong men No. 5.

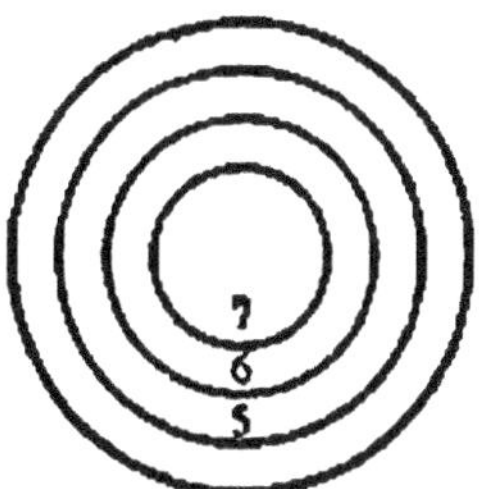


This division does not concern us at the moment. For us, the three inner circles form one inner circle.

The outer circle in which we live has several names designating its different features. It is called the mechanical circle, because everything *happens* there, everything is mechanical and the people who live there are *machines*. It is also called the *circle of the confusion of tongues*, because people who live in this circle all speak in different languages and *never understand one another*. Everyone understands everything differently.

We have come to a very interesting definition of understanding. It is something that belongs to the inner circle of humanity and does not belong to us at all.

If men in the outer circle realise that they do not understand one another, and if they feel the need of understanding, they must try to penetrate into the inner circle, because understanding between people is possible only there.

Schools of different kinds serve as gates through which people can pass into the inner circles. But this penetration into the circle higher in comparison with the one in which a man is born requires long and difficult work. The very first step in this work is this study of a new language. You may ask: What is this language we are studying?

And now I am able to answer you.

It is the language of the inner circle, the language in which people can understand one another.

You must realise that standing, so to speak, outside the inner circle we can know only the rudiments this language. But even these rudiments will help us to understand one another better than we could ever understand without them.

The three inner circles have each a language of their own. We are studying the language of the outer of the inner circles. People in the outer-inner circle study the language of the middle circle, and people in the middle circle study the language of the innermost circle. If you ask me how all this can be proved I will answer that it can be proved only by further study of oneself and further observation. If we find that with the study of the system we can understand ourselves and other people, or for instance, certain books, or certain ideas *better* than we could understand them before, and particularly if we find definite facts which show that this *new* understanding develops, that will be, if not proof, at least a sign of the possibility of proof.

We must remember that our understanding, exactly as our consciousness, is not always on the same level. It is always moving up and down. That means that at one moment we understand more, and at another moment we understand less. If we notice these differences of understanding in ourselves, we shall be able to realise that there is a possibility first, of keeping to those higher levels of understanding and second, of surpassing them.

But theoretical study is not sufficient. You must work on your being and on the change of your being.

If you formulate your aim from the point of view that you wish to understand other people, you must remember one very important school principle: you can understand other people only as much as you understand yourself and *only on the level of your own being.*

This means that you can judge other people's knowledge, but you cannot judge their being. You can see in them only as much as you have in yourself. But people always make the mistake of thinking that they can judge other people's being. In reality, if they wish to meet and *understand* people of higher development than themselves they must work with the aim of changing their being.

Now we must return to the study of centres and to the study of attention and self-remembering, *because these are the only ways to understanding.*

Besides the division into two parts, positive and negative which, as we saw, is not the same in different centres, each of the four centres is divided into three parts. These three parts correspond to the definition of centres themselves. The first part is "mechanical" including moving and instinctive principles, or one of them predominating; the second is "emotional" and the third is "intellectual." The following diagram shows the position of parts in the intellectual centre.

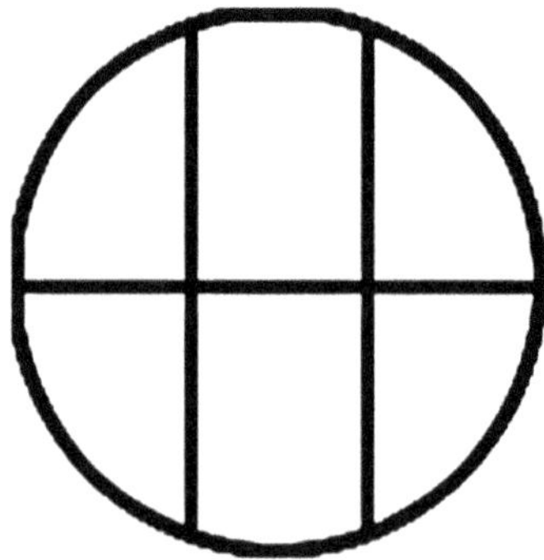

The centre is divided into positive and negative parts, each of these two parts is divided into three parts. Thus the Intellectual centre actually consists of six parts.

Each of these six parts is in its turn sub-divided into three parts: mechanical, emotional and intellectual. But about this sub-division we shall speak much later with the exception of one part, that is, the mechanical part of the intellectual centre, about which we shall speak presently.

The division of a centre into three parts is very simple. A mechanical part works almost automatically; *it does not require any attention*. But because of this it cannot adapt itself to a change of circumstances, it cannot "think" and it continues to work in the way it started when circumstances have completely changed.

In the intellectual centre, the mechanical part includes in itself all the work of registration of impressions, memories and associations. This is all that it should do normally, that is, when other parts do their work. It should never *reply* to questions addressed to the whole centre, it should never try to solve its problems, and it should never decide anything. Unfortunately, in actual fact, it is always ready to decide and it always replies to questions of all sorts in a very narrow and limited way, in ready-made phrases, in slang expressions, in party slogans. All these, and many other elements of our usual reactions, are the work of the mechanical part of the intellectual centre.

This part has its own name. It is called a "formatory apparatus" or sometimes "formatory centre." Many people, particularly people No. 1, that is, the great majority of mankind, live all their lives with the formatory apparatus only, never touching other parts of their intellectual centre. For all the immediate needs of life, for receiving A influences and responding to them, and for distorting or rejecting influences C, the formatory apparatus is quite sufficient.

It is always possible to recognise "formatory thinking." For instance, the formatory centre can count only up to two. It always divides everything in two: "bolshevism and fascism," "workers and bourgeois," "proletarians and capitalists" and so on. We owe most modern catchwords to formatory thinking, and not only catchwords but in modern popular theories. Perhaps it is possible to say that at all times all popular theories are formatory.

The emotional part of the intellectual centre consists chiefly of what is called an *intellectual emotion*, that desire to know, desire to understand, satisfaction of knowing, dissatisfaction of not knowing, pleasure of discovery and so on, although again all these can manifest themselves on very different levels.

The work of the emotional part requires full attention but in this *part of the centre attention does not require any effort.* It is attracted and held by the subject itself, very often through identification, which usually is called "interest," or "enthusiasm," or "passion," or "devotion".

The intellectual part of the intellectual centre includes in itself a capacity for creation, construction, invention and discovery. It cannot work without attention, but *the attention in this part of the centre must be controlled and kept there by will and effort.*

This is the chief criterion in studying parts of centres. If we take them from the point of view of *attention* we shall know at once in which part of centres we are. Without attention or with attention wandering, we are in the mechanical part: with the attention attracted by the subject of observation or reflection and kept there, we are in the emotional part; with the attention controlled and held on the subject by will, we are in the intellectual part.

At the same time, the same method shows how to make the intellectual parts of centres work. By observing attention and trying to control it, we compel ourselves to work in the intellectual parts of centres, because the same principle refers to all centres equally, although it may not be so easy for us to distinguish intellectual parts in other centres, as for instance the intellectual part of instinctive centre, which works without any attention that we can perceive or control.

Let us take the emotional centre. I will not speak at present about negative emotions. We will take only the division of the centre into three parts: mechanical, emotional and intellectual.

The *mechanical* part consists of the cheapest kind of ready-made humour and a rough sense of the comical, love of excitement, love of spectacular shows, love of pageantry, sentimentality, love of being in a crowd and part of a crowd; attraction to crowd emotions of all kinds and complete disappearance in lower half-animal emotions: cruelty, selfishness, cowardice, envy, jealousy, and so on.

The *emotional* part may be very different in different people. It may include in itself a sense of humour or a sense of the comical as well as religious emotion, aesthetic emotion, moral emotion and, in this case, it may lead to the awakening of *conscience*. But with identification it may be something quite different, it may be very ironical, sarcastic, derisive, cruel, obstinate, wicked and jealous – only in a less primitive way than the mechanical part.

The *intellectual* part of the emotional centre (with the help of the intellectual parts of the moving and instinctive centres) includes in itself the power of artistic creation. In those cases where the intellectual parts of the moving and instinctive centres which are necessary for the manifestation of the creative faculty are not sufficiently educated or do not correspond to it in their development, it may manifest itself in dreams. This explains the beautiful and artistic dreams of otherwise quite unartistic people.

The intellectual part of the emotional centre is also the chief seat of the magnetic centre. I mean that if magnetic centre exists only in the intellectual centre or in the emotional part of the emotional centre, it cannot be strong enough to be effective and is always liable to make mistakes or fail. But the intellectual part of the emotional centre, when it is fully developed and works with its full power, is a way to higher centres.

In the moving centre, the mechanical part is automatic. All automatic movements which in ordinary language are called "instinctive" belong to it, as well as imitation and the capacity for imitation which plays such a big part in life.

The emotional part of the moving centre is connected chiefly with the pleasure of movement. Love of sport and of games should *normally* belong to this part of the moving centre, but when identification and other emotions become mixed with it, it is very rarely there, and in most cases the love of sport is in the moving part of either the intellectual or the emotional centres.

The intellectual part of the moving centre is a very important and a very interesting instrument. Everyone who has ever done *well* any kind of physical work, whatever it may have been, knows that every kind of work needs many *inventions*. One has to *invent* one's own small methods for everything one does. These inventions are the work of the intellectual part of the moving centre, and many other inventions of man also need the work of the intellectual part of the moving centre. The power of imitating *at will* the voice, intonations and gestures of other people, *such as actors possess,* also belongs to the intellectual part of moving centre; but in higher or better degrees it is mixed with the work of the intellectual part of the emotional centre.

The work of the instinctive centre is very well hidden from us. We really know, that is, feel and can observe, only the sensory and emotional part.

The mechanical part includes in itself habitual sensations which very often we do not notice at all, but which serve as a background to other sensations; also *instinctive movements* in the correct meaning of the expression, that is, all inner movements such as the circulation of the blood, the movement of food in the organism and inner and outer reflexes.

The intellectual part is very big and very important. In the state of self-consciousness or approaching it, one can come into contact with the intellectual part of the Instinctive centre and learn a great deal from it concerning the functioning of the machine and its possibilities. The intellectual part of the instinctive centre is the mind behind all the work of the organism, a mind quite different from the intellectual mind.

The study of parts of centres and their special functions requires a certain degree of self-remembering. Without remembering oneself one cannot observe for a sufficiently long time or sufficiently clearly to feel and understand the difference of functions belonging to different parts of different centres.

The study of attention shows the parts of centres better than anything, but the study of attention again requires a certain degree of self-remembering.

Very soon you will realise that all your work upon yourself is connected with self-remembering and that it cannot proceed successfully without this. And self-remembering is *partial awakening,* or the beginning of awakening. Naturally – and this must be very clear – *no work can be done in sleep.*

# LECTURE HELD THURSDAY, 23 SEPTEMBER 1937

There are some things I want to speak about, because without understanding them you will not be able to understand many other things.

First of all, we must talk about schools, then about the principles and methods of the organisation and work of schools, and particularly about rules, then about the history of our work. Soon you will be able to read the beginning of a book I am writing, called *Fragments of an Unknown Teaching* (now titled *In Search of the Miraculous*), where I describe how I met this system and how the work developed.

It was explained to you many times and in different ways that nobody can work alone without a school. Also it must be clear to you by now that a group of people who decide to work by themselves will arrive nowhere, because they do not know *where to go and what to do.* The question arises. What is a school? And the next question which is most important for us is: Is *this* i.e., our organisation, a school?

There are many kinds of schools. I have spoken before about the four ways: way of fakir, way of monk, way of yogi and the fourth way. From the point of view of this division schools are also divided in the four kinds: fakir schools, religious schools or monasteries yogi schools and the schools of the fourth way.

Then – what constitutes a school? Speaking generally, a school is a place where one can learn something, i.e., from the school. There can be schools of modern languages, schools of music, schools of medicine, etc. But the kind of school I mean is not only for learning but also for becoming different. A school I speak about must not only give knowledge but also help to change being: without that it would be just an ordinary school. Knowledge is necessary, but knowledge can come only from those who passed *the same way before*. So the man who can conduct work must come from a school; that means he must be connected with a school, or at least he must have received instruction from a school in the past. A self-appointed or elected head of a group also cannot lead it anywhere.

Then schools are divided by degrees. There are schools where men No. 1, 2, and 3 learn how to become No. 4 and acquire all the knowledge that will help them in this change. The next degree are schools where men No. 4 learn how to become No. 5. There is no need for us to speak of further degrees, as they are too far from us.

Now an interesting question arises: Can we call ourselves a school? In a certain sense we may, because we acquire a certain knowledge and at the same time learn how to change our being. But I must say in relation to this that in the beginning of our work, i.e., in 1916 in St. Petersburg, we understood that a school, in the full sense of the term, *must consist of two degrees*, i.e., it must have two levels in it, one level where men No 1, 2, and 3 learn to become No. 4, and the other where men No. 4 learn to become No. 5. If a school has two levels it has more possibilities, because a double organisation of this kind can give a larger variety of experience and make the work more quick and more sure. So, although in a certain sense we can call ourselves a school, it is better to use this term for a bigger organisation.

What makes a school? First of all, it is understanding of principles of school work and discipline of a certain very definite kind connected with rules. When people come to lectures, they are told about certain rules they must keep. These rules are the conditions on which they are accepted and given knowledge. Keeping these rules or conditions is their first payment.

The first rule I was told about was that I must promise not to write about anything I hear. Later you will hear what I answered when I was told this and how this problem was solved. This rule means that you cannot write, without the permission of the person conducting the work from whom you have learned, what you intend to write, and when you write, if you get his permission, you must refer to the man from whom you learnt these ideas, and to the source of these ideas.

When I publish the *Fragments* you will be able to write. So long as *Fragments* is not published you cannot write. When this book is published, this condition will be removed, but not until then.

Then there are other rules: you must not talk. This means you must not make these ideas subject of ordinary talk, without aim or purpose. And if you talk with a certain aim and a certain purpose – I mean with people outside of the work – you must be very careful and you must not say much. You must remember that people *must pay* for what they hear. This is the principle of the work, and you have no right to give ideas to people for which they not only not pay but even cannot be expected to pay. It is better to ask permission to speak in each individual case.

Now I want to speak about one particular rule that was introduced into these groups and which is very important. I must explain how this rule arose, and before this, I must give you a short description of the history of the work. I met this system in 1915 in Russia. There was a group in Moscow conducted by G. I. Gurdjieff, a Caucasian Greek who came to Russia from Central Asia. I learned very much working with these groups, but in 1918 I parted from them because from my point of view they began to lose the most important of their original principles. Soon after my parting with them almost all members of groups parted with Mr. G. Only four people remained with him.

I met Mr. G. again in 1920 at Constantinople and again tried to work with him, but very soon found that it was impossible. In the beginning of 1922 when I was already in London Mr. G. came to me and told me about his plans for new work which he intended to start in England or in France. I did not believe much in these plans, but I decided to make a last experiment and promised to help him to organise his work. At that time I already had groups in London. After some time G.'s work was started in France. I collected money for him and many of my people went to the place he bought at Fontainebleau on their money. I went there myself several times and continued to do it till the end of 1923, when I saw that things were going wrong at Fontainebleau and decided to part with Mr. G. completely.

If you ask me what was wrong, I can say only one thing, which really was quite sufficient to wreck everything. By this time Mr. G. had abandoned most of the principles he himself taught us in Russia, particularly principles referring to choice and preparation of people for the work. He began to accept people without any preparation, gave them places of authority, permitted them to speak about the work and so on. I saw that his work was going to crash, and I parted with him in order to save the work in London.

In January 1924 I told my groups in London that I had broken all connections with Mr. G. and his group and would continue my work on my own as I began it in 1921. I offered them free choice: to remain with me or to follow Mr. G. or to leave the work altogether. At the same time, for those who decided to remain with me I introduced a new rule, namely, that they should not speak about Mr. G. or discuss the causes of the failure of the work at Fontainebleau. I introduced this rule because I wished to stop imagination, for since nobody knew anything, all talks on these subjects would have been pure invention or repetition of malignant gossiping, which came from Mr. G.'s new people, and who from my point of view, should not have been admitted in the work at all. I said that whoever wishes to know anything about it, he must ask me.

This rule remains and it was never revoked, but people never properly understood it and made all sort of excuses for themselves, or even affirmed that this rule was for other people but not for them. You must understand that all rules are for self-remembering. First, they have a purpose in themselves, and second they are for self-remembering. There are no rules that are not for self-remembering, although in themselves they may have a different aim. If there are no rules, there is no work. If the importance of rules is not understood, the possibilities of a school disappears.

*Miss F*: Why do you say that it is worse to talk about the system without mentioning where you got it from?

*Mr. Ouspensky*: Because speaking about it without mentioning the source of your information would be stealing. For instance, you cannot take ideas from a book and not mention the book. People only do this with my books; they constantly steal ideas from my books.

*Mr. M*: How long had the Moscow school existed?

*Mr. Ouspensky*: Several years in Moscow.

*Mr. M*: What was its size?

*Mr. Ouspensky*: This is neither here nor there. Before that, it existed in Central Asia. As for how long it had existed before – there are reasons to believe that it took this form and was formulated in this language in the beginning of the nineteenth century.

*Mr. M*: Does this knowledge claim to have connection with esoteric knowledge?

*Mr. Ouspensky*: Obviously, otherwise it would have no meaning. A school can only start from another school, otherwise it would be just a formatory invention.

*Mr. M*: So it is an unbroken chain?

*Mr. Ouspensky*: It must be, although you cannot trace it. You can only trace certain connections by ideas and terminology. This system came from the East; yet it has European terminology. In terminology it is connected, evidently through Russian masons of the eighteenth century with several earlier authors, for instance, with Dr. Fludd.

*Miss J*: You said you will tell us in what sense we can call this a school.

*Mr. Ouspensky*: I think I have answered it. Only a two-degree school is reliable. Another school may be a school today and not a school tomorrow, as happened with the Moscow school. Also, long ago I explained that an organisation which is a school for one person is not a school for another. Much depends on personal attitude and personal work.

*Miss R*. If schools are a real living thing, why do they die?

*Mr. Ouspensky*: What do you mean, saying that schools are living beings? It is vague and indefinite. But if we take it literally, it will make quite clear why schools die. All living things die sooner or later. If people die, schools also must die. It was explained in my lectures that a school needs certain conditions. If these conditions are destroyed, the school is destroyed. If there was a school in Canton or Wanhsien, it could be destroyed now and it would cease to exist.

*Miss R*: Ideas may remain?

*Mr. Ouspensky*: Ideas cannot fly. They need human heads. And a school does not consist of ideas. You forget all the time that a school teaches how to improve our being.

*Mr. F*: No ideas were written down in the past?

*Mr. Ouspensky*: Maybe, but ideas can be written down in different forms; they may be written down so that nobody can read them without explanation from those who know or without change of being. Take the Gospels – they are written in different ciphers. One must know the key to decipher them. Otherwise it would be just a story, doubtful historically and producing many wrong effects.

*Mr. F*: Will the system give the key to the Gospels?

*Mr. Ouspensky*: Some keys, but you cannot expect all the keys. Many keys can be got only with the change of being; they cannot be only a matter of knowledge. Again you forget about being. Change of being means connection with higher centres. Higher centres can understand many things which ordinary centres cannot understand.

*Mr. F*: Is a school self-evolving?

*Mr. Ouspensky*: What do you mean by this? If your question refers to origin of schools, then they are not self-evolving because one school must always start from another school.

*Mr. F*: Can a school reach a higher level than the school it started from?

*Mr. Ouspensky*: Yes, if it works according to methods and principles of school work, it can grow. But you must remember that the level of the school depends on the level of being of people who constitute it.

*Mr. F*: You said one can learn how to escape only from those who have escaped before.

*Mr. Ouspensky*: Quite right, in the allegory of prison. And this means a school can start only from another school.

*Mrs. D*: Would it be possible for everyone in a school to progress from No. 4 to No. 5, or only for a few?

*Mr. Ouspensky*: There is no limitation in principle. But you must understand that there is an enormous difference between No. 4 and No. 5. Man No. 4 is a man who has acquired a permanent centre of gravity, but in everything else he is an ordinary man. Man No. 5 is very different. He already has unity, he has permanent "I," he has the third state of consciousness, i.e., self-consciousness. That means he is awake, he can always when he needs remember himself, and the higher emotional centre works in him, and this gives him many new powers.

*Mrs. D:* The idea then is to attempt to get to No. 5?

*Mr. Ouspensky*: First you must think of how to become man No. 4, otherwise it will be just fantasy.

*Mrs. S*: Has man No. 4 less "I"s?

*Mr. Ouspensky*: Maybe he has more, but he has better control of them.

*Mr. A*: The chief immediate objectives you recommend are elimination of emotional life?

*Mr. Ouspensky*: No, quite different; emotional life is most important. The system speaks of elimination of negative emotions. Negative emotions are an intermediate state between sanity and insanity. A man whose centre of gravity is in negative emotions cannot be called sane and cannot develop. He must become normal first.

*Mr. A*: Why I spoke of the elimination of emotional life was because you said that all our emotions are potentially negative.

*Mr. Ouspensky*: Yes, potentially, but it does not mean that they all become negative. Emotional centre is the most important in us for our development. There are many things one can understand only with emotional centre. Intellectual centre is very limited, it cannot take us very far. The future belongs to the emotional centre.

But it must be understood that negative emotions are not really in the emotional centre. They are controlled by an artificial centre, and this is our only chance of getting rid of them. If their centre was *real* and not artificial, there would be no chance of getting rid of them, because it would mean that they are useful, or may be useful, in some way. The artificial centre is created by a long wrong work of the machine. There is nothing useful about it. Because of this, negative emotions can be eliminated; they do not serve any useful purpose.

*Mrs. S*: So none of us use the emotional centre rightly?

*Mr. Ouspensky:* Why not?

*Mrs. S*: You said we have no positive emotions.

*Mr. Ouspensky*: Positive emotions are quite a different thing, they belong to the higher emotional centre. Man No. 5 has positive emotions. All our emotions can become negative, although, as I said, it does not mean every emotion *will* become negative. At the same time, our emotions are not reliable so long as there is no control and so long as we are asleep. But they will become more and more reliable if we become less asleep and acquire more control.

*Mr. D*: Does a school suffer if a member breaks a rule?

*Mr. Ouspensky*: It depends how important was the rule. By breaking a rule he may break the school. Or the man who conducts the school may close it if certain rules are broken.

*Mr. F*: You say that a school which embraces two degrees is more effective. How can one part of it be allied to the other?

*Mr. Ouspensky*: You can only learn this by practice. If a school has two degrees it has much more powers.

*Mrs. B*: Does this system exist in other European countries?

*Mr. Ouspensky*: I never heard.

*Mr. M*: Has communal life to do with the organisation of schools?

*Mr. Ouspensky*: It depends what kind of communal life you mean. For instance, some time ago in Russia existed so-called Tolstoy Colonies. Most of them had the same history. People decided to live together, bought some land and so on, then after the first three days they began to quarrel and it all came to nothing.

*Mr. M*: I meant a group of people who live in the same building.

*Mr. Ouspensky*: It depends first of all on the condition *by whom* it is organised. If it is organised by themselves, it generally comes to nothing. But if a school organises itself according to definite principles and with definite rules – in some cases it may be useful.

*Miss R*: Has the man who organises a school authority?

*Mr. Ouspensky*: He has responsibility, so he must have authority.

*Miss R*: Where does it come from?

*Mr. Ouspensky*: From his knowledge, from his understanding, from his being.

*Question*: Not to be able to go on with the system is worse than not to have started?

*Mr. Ouspensky*: If you have started, nobody can stop you except yourself.

*Mr. M*: How to reconcile this with what you have said about there being no guarantee?

*Mr. Ouspensky*: It depends on your work. How can I guarantee your work?

*Mr. M*: But facilities for work would remain? I mean if a person works.

*Mr. Ouspensky*: Barring catastrophes. We live in insecure times. About guarantee – what we can get depends on our own efforts and one must work at one's own risk. But after some time one begins to see: "I got this that I did not have before" and "I got that that I did not have before." So little by little one can be more sure.

*Mr. A*: I suppose also you can give no guarantee as to whether people will suffer from some delusion as regards personal experience? One may take illusion for fact?

*Mr. Ouspensky*: Yes, very easy, but if one remembers all that one was told, one learns to discriminate.

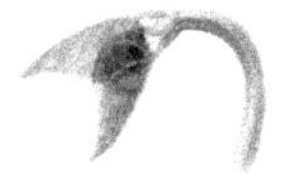

# NOTES ON DECISION TO WORK

Think very seriously before you decide to work on yourself with the idea of changing yourself, i.e. to work with the definite aim of becoming conscious and of developing connection with higher centres. This work admits of no compromise and it requires a great amount of self-discipline and readiness to obey all rules and particularly, direct instructions.

Think very seriously: are you really ready and willing to obey, and do you fully understand the necessity for it? There is no going back. If you agree and then go back, you will lose everything that you have acquired up to that time, and you will lose more really, because all that you acquired will turn into something wrong in you. There is no remedy against this.

Understanding of the necessity for obeying rules and direct instructions must be based on the realization of your mechanicalness and your helplessness. If this realization is not strong enough, you had better wait and occupy yourself with ordinary work; study of the system, work in groups, etc. If you do this work sincerely and remember all rules, it will bring you to the realization of your state and your needs. But you must not delay too long. If you want to come to real work you must hurry. You must understand that the opportunity that exists today may not come your way again. You may lose all your chances by hesitating and waiting too long.

If you decide to work and accept all that comes in the work, you must learn to think quickly. If you are offered a task you must answer at once that you accept it. If you hesitate or take time to answer, the offer of the task will be withdrawn and it will not be repeated. You may be given time before actually doing what you were told to do, but you must accept the task at once. An attempt to talk things over, an ironical, suspicious or negative attitude, fear, or lack of confidence, these will make the task impossible at once. If you feel hesitation about the task offered to you, think about your mechanicalness, think about your negativeness, about your self-will – but think quickly. You can do nothing against your weak sides by yourself. The tasks offered to you have the aim of helping you. If you hesitate of refuse them, you refuse help. This must be quite clear in your mind.

The realization of your helplessness and your deep sleep must be permanent in you. You can strengthen it by constantly reminding yourself of your nothingness, of your meanness, of your weakness of all possible sorts. You have absolutely nothing to be proud of. You have nothing to base your judgement on. You can see, if you are sincere with yourself, all the blunders and all the mistakes which you made when you tried to act by yourself. You cannot think rightly. You cannot feel rightly. You need constant help, and you can have it. But you must pay for it – at least, by not arguing.

You have to do gigantic work if you want to become different. How can you ever hope to get anything if you hesitate and argue on the first steps, or do not even realize the necessity for help, or become suspicious and negative?

If you want to work seriously you have to conquer many things in yourself. You cannot carry with yourself your prejudices, your fixed opinions, your personal identifications or animosities.

But at the same time try to understand that personal is

not always wrong. Personal can even help in the work but personal can be very dangerous too, if it is not cleared by the struggle with identification and by the realization of your mechanicalness and your weakness.

Try to understand the necessity for deliberate suffering and conscious effort. These are the only two things that can change you and bring you to your aim.

Deliberate suffering does not mean necessary suffering inflicted on you by yourself. It means attitude towards suffering. Suffering may come as a result of your feeling, thoughts and actions connected with your task; it may come by itself as a result of your own faults or as a result of other people's actions, attitudes or feelings. But what is important is your attitude towards it. It becomes deliberate if you do not rebel against it, if you do not try to avoid it, if you do not accuse anybody, if you accept it as a necessary part of your work at the moment, and as a means for attaining your aim.

Conscious effort is the effort based on understanding; understanding of its necessity first of all, and understanding of causes which make it necessary. The chief cause for conscious effort is your need for breaking the walls of mechanicalness, of self-will and of lack of self-remembering which constitute your being at present.

In order to understand better the necessity for accepting tasks given to you without hesitation, the necessity for deliberate suffering and conscious effort, think about ideas which brought you to the work, think about the first realization of your mechanicalness and the first realization that you know nothing. In the beginning you realized this and you came for help, but now you doubt whether you must really do as you are told. And you try to find ways to evade it, to stand on your own judgement and on your own understanding. You understood clearly once, that your judgement and your understanding are false and weak, but now you try to keep them again. You do not want to give them up. Well, you can keep them, but you must understand that with them you will keep all that is false and weak in yourself. There are no half measures. You must decide. Do you want to work or not?

# NOTES ON WORK ON ONESELF

Try to remember and keep in your mind constantly all the lines on which you have to work. You have to work on mind, on consciousness, on emotions and on will. Try to understand that each line of work needs special attention, special methods and special understanding. After some time all four will begin to help one another and later they will merge into one, but in the beginning the four lines must go separately.

Try to understand the work on *mind.* To do this work you must constantly revise all ideas of the system referring to man and the universe, and particularly those referring to psychology, the study of emotions, many "I"s, the division of man, false personality, permanent "I", esotericism, schools and methods of school work. Keep your mind on these ideas or at least return to them as often as possible. Your mind must never be idle. At every possible moment you must reflect on one or another idea, on one or another aspect of the system and methods.

Try to understand the necessity for introducing the methods and principles of the work in your *personal life* and first of all the necessity for right thinking on all personal questions and their possible relation to your work. Without this, you will never reach unity. You cannot allow one part of yourself to think wrongly and hope that another part will think rightly.

Understanding of principles, rules and methods of school work is one of the most important parts of the work on mind. Mind must be trained not to hesitate in its choice between right and wrong, must understand perfectly right relations to me, to other people in the work and to the people outside.

Mind must understand that in the very beginning of serious work on oneself one gives up one's freedom. Certainly it is an illusionary freedom, but when one puts oneself under the laws of the work, one is naturally under more laws than someone outside the work.

Try to understand the meaning of *silence* in the work, the meaning of *sincerity* and the meaning of *truth*.

One can never expect to get anything from the work if one cannot keep silence when it is not necessary to speak for the sake of the work. People generally talk too much, talk for their own gratification, from self-pride, from vanity, from desire to live again through pleasant or painful experiences; they talk because they cannot resist identification with talking or because they do not realize that they should not talk in this particular way or on this particular subject. Very often the special attraction of talking, for them, is in the fact that they know that they should not talk.

I do not even mean talking to people outside the work. That must have been dealt with long before any possibility of serious work on oneself arises.

What I mean is that one must be very guarded even in speaking to one's friends in the work, unless one is told by me to speak.

Also, one cannot expect anything if one cannot be sincere with oneself and with me. With other people in the work one can have a mutual arrangement regarding sincerity about everything or about particular subjects, but this can only be done with my approval and with my complete knowledge of what is said.

Further, one cannot expect to get anything from the work if one is afraid or reluctant to speak the truth to me even without being told to do so.

You must understand that nobody who wishes to remain in the work can ask another person in the work to keep something from me, and nobody can give the promise to keep anything secret. This is a very important point.

One must always be ready to tell me anything about oneself and anything one may learn about another person. And one must do so by oneself without being reminded, and do it with full understanding that this is an essential part of the work.

You must understand that you cannot accept part of the rules and reject or forget another part. You must understand the importance of discipline in the work.

You must understand the meaning of the words: *sacrifice your suffering*, and the right moments, right methods and the aim and possible results of such sacrifice.

You must understand the necessity for being careful when saying "I". You can say "I" when speaking about yourself only when you are sure that you speak about work or ideas or rules and principles of the work, in accordance with all rules and principles. In all other cases you must try to understand which part of you is speaking or thinking, and name it accordingly. This idea must not be exaggerated. You can say without harm: I am going to buy some cigarettes. But you cannot say: I dislike this man. You must find which part of you dislikes him and why, and not ascribe this dislike to all of you.

You must clearly understand the necessity of self-observation for self-study. You must understand the difference between functions and consciousness. Thinking of functions, you must always be able to distinguish the intellectual, emotional, moving and instinctive function; positive and negative parts of centres in the intellectual and instinctive centres; moving, emotional and intellectual parts in all centres. You must study attention and understand how, by the study of attention, you can distinguish parts of centres.

In relation to the study of *consciousness* you must remember what you know about sleep and waking state, the different levels in waking state, and the connection of higher centres with higher states of consciousness. You must remember that your aim is to establish connection with higher centres. You must understand that higher centres have many unknown functions which cannot be described in ordinary language. They have much more power, and a deeper penetration into the laws of nature. You must remember that many problems insoluble for our ordinary mind can become soluble for higher centres. And you must always return to the idea of permanent "I" and realize how far you are from it and how many efforts and sacrifices are necessary in order to reach it.

In the work on *consciousness* you must understand first of all, that this work is entirely practical. Theoretical study will not help. Second, you must understand that the work on consciousness can give results only when it becomes permanent or as near to permanent as possible. Spasmodic, accidental, interrupted work cannot give results. So try to find how you can make your work on consciousness continuous. Your mind must guide you in the beginning, constantly reminding you of the necessity for remembering yourself, and helping you to catch the moments of not remembering.

But realize that mind can only *prepare* you for this work and only guide you for a certain distance. You can go further in the work on consciousness only with the help of will and emotions.

Remember also, that consciousness can be measured by the length of periods of consciousness and by the frequency of the appearance of these periods.

Efforts to create consciousness in oneself feel almost hopeless in the beginning. But very soon they will begin to give results. You will notice these results by observing moments of consciousness appearing by themselves without any effort on your part. In reality, they are the results of previous efforts.

The practice of stopping thoughts helps self-remembering very much. Struggle with imagination and with mechanical talk with oneself or with people is necessary from the very beginning. But one will get still stronger help for self-remembering from sacrificing one's suffering. Only this can make the work on consciousness real and serious. Before this, all is only preparation for it.

The work on *emotions* as the work on consciousness must be practical from the beginning. It begins with the struggle against the expression of negative emotions. When a certain control is acquired and when you fully understand all evil sides of negative emotions in your own life and in life in general, you must make a plan for your personal work on identification, imagination and lying in those particular forms which they take in you.

In this work you must not be afraid to hurt yourself. Understand that only by hurting yourself can you get what you want. You can do this by observing rules. For instance, by saying something about yourself or about other people that you do not want to say, but when you are told to do so. Also, you can produce a very emotional state in yourself by preparing yourself to speak in this way, that is, by imagining yourself being told to speak the truth on the most difficult and intimate subjects which you think are quite hidden or disguised.

Realize also, that there are many other kinds of suffering through which you will pass before you attain your aim. Try to understand that suffering is *the only active principle in us* which can be converted into higher feeling – which is also higher thought and higher understanding.

Do not be afraid of thinking of your emotions and finding contradictions in them, even if it hurts you. Only be comparing different emotions referring to the same subject can you find buffers in yourself and eventually destroy them if you work hard enough and are not afraid of hurting yourself.

Remember that this will lead you to the awakening of conscience, which is the simultaneous feeling of all contradictory emotions; and remember that the awakening of conscience is a necessary step for transferring yourself to the higher level of consciousness.

Practice removing identification and imagination from negative emotions without destroying them. You may get quite unexpected and very interesting results.

Learn to transform emotions into mental attitudes and to transfer them to the mind. Many emotions which are quite useless and even harmful in emotional centre, because they cannot exist there without identification and imagination, become quite useful as mental attitudes and help self-observation, observation of other people and general understanding.

Try to go through all your emotions during all the time you have been connected with the system, emotions referring to the system itself, to me, to yourself and to other people in the work.

Try to be sincere with yourself. See how you have always tried to profit by your being in the work; for instance, by using the particular intimacy that establishes itself between people in the work, owing to common psychological study and the disappearance of many buffers, for making friends in the ordinary mechanical and sentimental way, having love affairs, etc. See what use you have made of your connection with the work. See how you were often selfish and calculating, how little you gave to the work and how much you took from it. See how much considering was in your attitudes, how many demands and how much resentment, particularly when people tried to help you. Try to see how poor was your valuation of the work and how much you missed by it. Try to see how foolish you were to express negative opinions of people who could have helped you, many of whom have disappeared already. Try to see yourself as you really are. And do not let yourself rest, do not comfort yourself with false hopes and expectations of miracles, or with decisions to act differently tomorrow.

Think about life in general, think about masses of blind and sleeping people without any chance in the world to become anything else. Think about yourself, realize how many opportunities you had and how many you have already lost and continue to lose daily.

Think about death. You do not know how much time remains to you. And remember that if you do not become different, everything will be repeated again, all foolish blunders, all silly mistakes, all loss of time and opportunity

– everything will be repeated with the exception of the *chance* you had this time, because *chance* never comes in the same form.

You will have to *look for* your chance next time. And in order to do this, you will have to remember many things, and how will you remember then if you do not remember anything now?

Try to understand the work on *will*. You begin this work by work on mind and consciousness; work on emotions strengthens will still more, and prepares you for further efforts. But real work on will begins with trying to understand self-will and finding examples of its manifestations in your actions. At this point comes the necessity for great sincerity with yourself and the necessity for being ready to speak to me about your manifestations of self-will. Try to understand that every decision made by yourself and for yourself which can at the same time affect your work is the manifestation of self-will.

In order to understand better the difference between will and self-will, learn to distinguish between mechanical and conscious. Self-will is always mechanical, will is always conscious. You must understand that even on an ordinary level there is a great difference between mechanical and conscious. In life the difference is connected with the difference between important and unimportant, but in life the difference between important and unimportant varies for different people and changes according to the change of circumstances. For people in schools, "important" is always connected with the work.

If you consider yourself connected with school work or wish to be in school work but hesitate in relation to life matters and do not know which way to choose, you can always find what is more important for you by looking at the question from this point of view.

"Important" is always, in one way or in many ways, connected with the work and cannot contradict principles and methods of the work. Mechanical decisions and mechanical actions always contradict the methods of the work, and harm your work and your position in the work.

If you cannot decide yourself what is more important and which way to choose, *you must ask me.*

If you are seriously in the work and want to be in the work, you must not make any decision which may affect your life without first asking my opinion. Your own decisions in serious cases are bound to be based on self-will.

But you cannot ask my opinion or my decision when your decision is already made and you have already begun to act on the basis of it, because that means self-will in action, and in such a case it is too late to ask me. Questions as to my opinion and my decision when your decision is already made, are really manifestations of insincerity with yourself and attempts to deceive me by false pretences.

Try to realize that mechanical actions and mechanical decisions are always based on considerations outside the work (even if you persuade yourself that the result will be useful for your work), considerations of pleasure, of convenience or comfort; or they result from negative emotions or imagination.

Try to understand that if you are in the work and wish to be in the work the most mechanical manifestation is lying to me or suppressing the truth from me.

Demand for complete truth does not refer to people only beginning to work with me. They must make long preliminary work on mind and consciousness before complete truth becomes necessary and obligatory. But when they realize the necessity for personal help, and when I find that they are ready and I can help them, the principle of complete truth becomes obligatory. And it is certainly obligatory for all people who have been in the work for five years and also for some who have been in the work much less but have already formulated their aim.

Remember that your chief work must be on self-will. One begins to give up one's self-will by accepting rules, but one must be sincere about it. Later one must give up one's self-will in all serious matters and accept another person's will, in this case, mine. Only by doing this, and doing it with full understanding of the necessity for doing so, one will begin to acquire slowly one's own will. Really, the very act of giving up one's self-will is the first act and the first manifestation of real will.

The four lines of work on oneself can be designated: intellectual work – *preparation*; work on consciousness – *aim*; work on emotions – *means*, *energy*; work on will – *control*, and also *energy*.

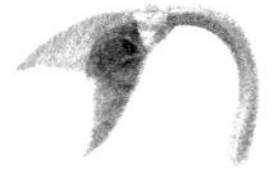

## WHAT IS SCHOOL?

*Question:* What is school?

*Ouspensky:* School is an organization for the transmission to a certain number of prepared people of knowledge coming from higher mind.

The most essential thing in school is the knowledge which comes from higher mind. This means that schools cannot be formed arbitrarily without the participation of people who have obtained knowledge in schools. Another very important fact is the selection effected by the school, that is, the selection of students. Only people of a certain preparation and a certain level of understanding are admitted. A school cannot be open to all, it cannot even be open to many. A school is always a closed circle with the instructor in the centre.

Schools can be of very different levels depending on the preparation and the level of being of the students. The higher the level of the school the greater the demands made upon the students.

*Question:* Why are schools necessary?

*Ouspensky:* Before speaking of *why* schools are necessary it must be realized *for whom* schools are necessary, because schools are not necessary at all for the vast majority of people. Schools are necessary to those people who already realize the inadequacy of knowledge collected by the ordinary mind and who feel that, by themselves, with their own strength they can neither resolve the problems which surround them nor find the right way. Only such people are capable of overcoming the difficulties connected with school work and only for them are schools necessary.

In order to understand *why* schools are necessary it must

be realized that the knowledge which comes from men of higher mind can be transmitted only to a very limited number of people simultaneously and with the necessary observance of a whole series of definite conditions which must be well known to the instructor of the school and without which knowledge cannot be transmitted *correctly*.

The existence of these conditions and the impossibility of doing without them explains the necessity of an organisation. The transmission of knowledge demands efforts both on the part of him who receives it and on the part of him who gives it. The organization facilitates these efforts or makes them possible. These conditions cannot come about by themselves. A school can only be organised according to a certain definite plan worked out and known long ago. There can be nothing arbitrary and improvised in schools. But schools can be of different type corresponding to different ways. Different ways will be spoken of later.

*Question:* Can it be explained in what these conditions consist?

*Ouspensky:* These conditions are connected with a definite property of man's nature, namely, that there are two sides of man which, in man's general development, ought to develop simultaneously and in parallel: *knowledge* and *being*. People know, or think they know, what knowledge is and to certain extent they understand the relativity of knowledge. But they do not know what being is and they do not understand the relativity of being and the fact that knowledge depends on being. Meanwhile the development of knowledge without corresponding development of being or a development of being without a corresponding development of knowledge gives wrong results. Schools are necessary in order to avoid such one-sided development and the undesirable results connected with it. The conditions of school teaching are such that from the very first steps work progresses simultaneously along two lines, along the line of knowledge and along the line of being. From the first days at school a man begins to study mechanicalness and to struggle against mechanicalness in himself, against involuntary actions, against unnecessary talk, against imagination, against day-dreaming and against sleep. It is explained to him that his knowledge depends on his being. In making one step along the line of knowledge a man must make a step along the line of being. The principles of school work, all the demands made upon him, the rules which he must remember, all help him to study his being and to work to change it.

*Question:* Why is knowledge necessary?

*Ouspensky:* The aim of a man who realizes his state and his position becomes a change of being. This change is so difficult that it would, in fact, be impossible if knowledge was not there to help him.

*Question:* Can a change of being, that is the attainment of a certain level of being, give knowledge?

*Ouspensky:* No, it cannot. Knowledge and being express two sides of man's nature which can develop and grow, but they require different efforts for their development.

*Question:* On what does understanding depend, on knowledge or on being?

*Ouspensky:* Neither knowledge nor being separately can give right understanding. The reason for this is that understanding is the resultant of knowledge and being. A growth of understanding is possible only with a simultaneous growth of knowledge and being. If one outgrows the other too much, understanding cannot develop in the right direction.

*Question:* What is meant by growth of knowledge and growth of being?

*Ouspensky:* The growth of knowledge means a transition from the particular to the general, from details to the whole, from the illusory to the real. Ordinary knowledge, or what is called knowledge, is always a knowledge of details without a knowledge of the whole, a knowledge of the leaves, or the veins and serrations in the leaves, without a knowledge of the tree. Real knowledge not only shows a given detail, but the place, the function and the meaning of this detail in the whole. In our ordinary knowledge there are times which bring us near to real knowledge. For instance, in the ordinary system of notation any number not only defines the power but shows the place of this power in the series of powers from zero to infinity. All real knowledge is of this nature.

Real knowledge comes from higher mind, that is, from the minds of men who have attained the fullest development possible for men. It is called *objective knowledge*, as distinct from the knowledge of ordinary men, which is called subjective knowledge. Objective knowledge is always *school* knowledge, that is, knowledge acquired in a school. A man cannot arrive at it with his own mind or get it from books.

One of the first ideas of objective knowledge is that a knowledge of the real world is possible, but only on the condition of being able to make use of the principles of *relativity* and *scale* and then of knowing the fundamental laws of the universe, the *law of three* and the *law of seven*. The approach to the study of objective knowledge begins with the study of an objective language. The next step is the study of oneself which begins with the understanding of man's place in the universe and the study of the human machine. The knowledge of oneself is both an aim and a means.

A man who has not had school teaching, that is, a man of a subjective way of thinking, lives surrounded by illusions, first of all about himself. He thinks that he has will and the possibility of choice every moment of his life; he thinks that he can *do*; he thinks that he has individuality, that is, something permanent and unchangeable; he thinks that he has an "I" or an Ego likewise permanent and unchangeable; he considers himself a *conscious being* and supposes that he is able to arrange life on earth by following indications of reason and logic; his usual state of consciousness, in which he lives and acts, he calls *clear consciousness* when in reality it is sleep. In this sleep he lives, writes books, invents theories, carries on wars, kills other sleeping people and dies himself without even suspecting for a moment that he can awake.

He does not realize the possibility of development or growth. He ascribes to himself that which he does not possess. But he does not know how much it is that he could acquire.

If he is a man of scientific views he does not admit the possibility of any individual evolution of man beyond the limits of ordinary intellectual development during life. Instead he acknowledges the possibility of the evolution of man *as a species* and he considers such evolution to be entirely mechanical, that is, not dependent upon anybody's will.

If he is a religious man he believes in a future life and that he is guided *for his own good* by higher powers with whom he can have intercourse by means of prayer.

If he is familiar with theosophy he believes in the law of Karma and in reincarnation; he considers that he has an astral body, a mental body and a causal body, and that through an inevitable evolution he will attain to the very highest degrees, if not on earth then on some other planet.

If he has already understood the inadequacy and the illusory nature of scientific, religious and theosophical ideas and realizes the necessity for inner change in man, he does not realize the difficulty of this, he does not realize the necessity for lengthy and systematic efforts which are impossible without a knowledge of methods and without an exact and detailed knowledge of the human machine. It seems to him that what *can* come *must* come.

But in reality nothing comes of itself. A man must first free himself from illusions and then work to attain another being. This work requires long and systematic efforts and knowledge.

*Question:* What is the difference between the school you speak of and the "esoteric school" in the Theosophical Society? It seems to me that the idea underlying both is identical.

*Ouspensky:* The principal difference between the school of which I speak and the "esoteric school" consists in the fact that the "esoteric school" is, so to speak, the superstructure or the upper story of the whole theosophy. In order to come to the "esoteric school" one must accept all the rest. And in the theosophical system there is very much that is naive, illogical, contradictory, and impossible.

*Question:* What is the difference between "Masters" and the beings of higher mind?

*Ouspensky:* "Masters" in theosophy are connected with a definite *legend* which begins with Blavatsky. In accepting

"Masters" you have to accept the whole legend. Meanwhile there is very much that is unacceptable and impossible in this legend. *People of higher mind* are not connected with any sort of legend. Man as we know him is regarded not as the highest possible expression of his kind and not as a completed being but as a being in a certain definite phase of his possible *transformation*. This transformation is considered to be possible in one lifetime, that is, it is considered that a man born in one phase can, during one lifetime, pass into another. If we take the example of a butterfly then man is approximately a caterpillar. And the vast majority of people die as "caterpillars." But out of the masses of caterpillars a small percentage of transforming beings is constantly emerging. These evolving beings are, for us, *people of higher mind*. We can know of their existence by traces of their activity in history, chiefly in art and in religions. Possessing a more perfect mind than ordinary people they possess greater knowledge. The schools of which I speak have as their aim to bring ordinary people, who have felt or realized the necessity of escaping from their present state, near to the ideas coming from people of higher mind, because these ideas alone can assist their transformation, that is, their transition to a new level of being.

*Question:* Do you think that beings such as the Buddha or the Christ had "school" knowledge?

*Ouspensky:* I cannot reply to the question about Christ and about Buddha because it must first be established what we accept and what we do not accept out of the legends connected with them. But if Christ really did exist then without doubt he taught his pupils *school science*. The Gospels are full of references to a school system and to school knowledge.

*Question:* The idea of initiation in the "esoteric school" is based on choice and appreciation of those who know better and that seems your idea too ("number of prepared people.")

*Ouspensky:* The idea of initiation depending on someone else has absolutely no place in the system. Only self-initiation exists, that is, inner growth. Only *knowledge* can be received from someone else and it cannot be received in any other way. Preparation means something quite different. In its first sense it is simply intellectual and emotional preparation giving a man the possibility of understanding and *valuing* new ideas. The necessity of preparation is emphasized only to show that the ideas of the system cannot be given to everybody without discrimination. Of the fuller significance of *preparation* I will speak later.

*Question:* There are a great many people who claim to belong to a school and to possess special knowledge. All of them say what you are saying. Where is the criterion to be found by which we will recognize the right man? The examples of some of these people seem much more to deny their knowledge than to affirm it.

Ouspensky: Of course, besides real schools there exist many false schools. The chief danger comes from schools possessing a very small amount of knowledge and a very large amount of fantasy, such as the theosophical, anthroposophical, martinist and so on. It is very difficult to indicate an exact criterion for making a discrimination on first acquaintance with a school, because such a criterion depends on the depth and the quality of preparation. For me personally the first proof of *this* school being right was an undoubted and exact knowledge in psychology surpassing everything I had ever heard before anywhere, and making psychology an exact and practical science. This was a fact, for me incontrovertible, and I had a special preparation for judging this fact.

Schools can be of very different levels.

1. Preparatory schools of the fourth way can be divided into two categories. To the first category belong schools whose instructor acknowledges *the superiority of his own being over the being of his students* and by this promises the student help which is based on the use of powers which surpass the powers of ordinary man. And to the second category belong schools whose instructor acknowledges the superiority only *of his knowledge*.

2. Schools of the first category, that is, schools whose instructor acknowledges the superiority of his being and his possession of powers which ordinary man does not possess, are incommensurably more difficult and it is only possible to be in them by *constantly* remembering the principles of the work, by making a *complete* submission to the instructor and by *strictly* keeping the rules. The slightest deviation from remembering principles, from submitting to the instructor and from keeping rules makes continuing study in such a school impossible.

3. In schools of the second category the instructor can excuse many failings of individual students, even though it delays their work, so long as it does no harm to the general work of the school.

4. Making the difficulties of the work easier, reducing the demands or making concessions on the part of the instructor is never a privilege or an advantage for the students, on the contrary, it always indicates only failure of their work and their loss of place in the work.

5. Only raising or increasing demands is a privilege.

6. Place in the work is determined by preparation, seniority, efforts, capacities, confidence in the instructor and understanding the aims of the work.

7. A student can begin without understanding fully the meaning of the ideas coming from higher mind and the aims of school work. But after a certain time a *right* valuation and understanding will be required of him and without this valuation and understanding he cannot continue.

8. The appearance of distrust towards the instructor and especially the expression of such distrust towards the knowledge, methods or personal opinions of the instructor makes continuing the work at the school impossible.

9. The student must remember that personal opinions of the instructor which contradicts his own personal opinions are based on better methods of observation and reasoning than those which he can have at his disposal. For him, therefore, they should be a subject of study, not a subject of argument or objection.

10. He must remember that one of the aims of his work is a change in his points of view because his old points of view – being the points of view of a sleeping man – cannot be right. The task of the instructor is to show him the possibility of points of view which are in accord and which, at the same time, will contribute to his awakening.

11. The student must remember that he came to learn and not to teach or express his views.

12. Difference of opinion with the instructor can be an indication that the student has already obtained from him everything he can obtain and that he ought to leave the school and work independently. At the same time difference

of opinion may simply show that the student has forgotten some of the fundamental principles of the work, or, what is still worse, has added something of his own to it, something he did not hear from the instructor. This makes all further work useless.

13. Independent work outside the school is possible in contact with the instructor or without contact.

14. Contact depends on the student and not on the instructor and is established if the student remembers everything that he has at any time heard from the instructor and follows all of it without any kind of deviation, and above all without adding anything of his own.

15. The instructor bears the responsibility for the work of the students and can help them in their difficulties only when in relation to him, they follow the principles of schools of the first category and submit to the rules of schools in the first category; that is, when they never forget what has once been said to them and do not argue with the instructor.

16. This is sometimes called *imitating school work*.

17. In one and the same school there can be different students, that is, students of schools of the first category and students of the second category. This difference between students is determined solely by their attitude towards the instructor.

– *finis* –

Aziloth Books publishes a wide range of titles ranging from hard-to-find esoteric books – *Parchment Books* – to classic works on fiction, politics and philosophy – *Cathedral Classics*. Our newest venture is *Aziloth Books Children's Classics*, with vibrant new covers and illustrations to complement some of the world's very best children's tales. All our imprints are offered to the reader at a competitive price and through as many mediums and outlets as possible.

We are committed to excellent book production and strive, whenever possible, to add value to our titles with original images, maps and author introductions. With the premium on space in most modern dwellings, we also endeavour – within the limits of good book design – to make our products as slender as possible, allowing more books to be fitted into a given bookshelf area.

We are a small, approachable company and would love to hear any of your comments and suggestions on our plans, products, or indeed on absolutely anything.

Aziloth Books, Rimey Law, Rookhope, Co. Durham, DL13 2BL, England.
t: 01388-517600 e: info@azilothbooks.com w: www.azilothbooks.com

Cathedral Classics hosts an array of classic literature, from erudite ancient tomes to avant-garde, twentieth-century masterpieces, all of which deserve a place in your home. All the world's great novelists are here, Jane Austen, Dickens, Conrad, Arthur Machen and Henry James, brushing shoulders with such disparate luminaries as Sun Tzu, Marcus Aurelius, Kipling, Friedrich Nietzsche, Machiavelli, and Omar Khayam. A small selection is detailed below:

| | |
|---|---|
| *Herland* | Charlotte Perkins Gilman |
| *The Rubaiyat of Omar Khayyam* | Omar Khayyam |
| *The Sign of the Four* | Arthur Conan Doyle |
| *The Picture of Dorian Gray* | Oscar Wilde |
| *Flatland* | Edwin A. Abbott |
| *The Coming Race* | Edward Bulwer-Lytton |
| *Beyond Good and Evil* | Friedrich Nietzsche |
| *The Genealogy of Morals* | Friedrich Nietzsche |
| *England, My England* | D. H. Lawrence |
| *The Castle of Otranto* | Horace Walpole |
| *Self-Reliance, & Other Essays* (series1&2) | Ralph W. Emmerson |
| *The Art of War* | Sun Tzu |
| *A Shepherd's Life* | W. H. Hudson |
| *To the Lighthouse; Mrs. Dalloway* | Virginia Woolf |
| *The Sorrows of Young Werther* | Johann W. Goethe |
| *Demian: the story of a youth* | Herman Hesse |
| *Analects* | Confucius |
| *The Subjection of Women* | John Stuart Mill |
| *Rights of Man* | Thomas Paine |
| *Progress and Poverty* | Henry George |
| *Captains Courageous* | Rudyard Kipling |
| *The Meditations of Marcus Aurelius* | Marcus Aurelius |
| *The Social Contract* | Jean Jacques Rousseau |
| *War is a Racket* | Smedley D. Butler |
| *The Dead* | James Joyce |
| *The Autobiography of Benjamin Franklin* | Benjamin Franklin |
| *Frankenstein or the Modern Prometheus* | Mary Shelley |
| *Anarchy* | Errico Malatesta |
| *The Interesting Narrative...Olaudah Equiano...* | Olaudah Equiano |
| *The History of Mary Prince, a West Indian slave* | Mary Prince |
| *The Strange Case of Dr. Jekyll & Mr. Hyde: Illus...* | Robert Louis Stevenson |
| *Imperialism, the Highest Stage of Capitalism...* | Vladimir Lenin |
| *The Prince: Translated by N. H. Thompson with...* | Niccolo Machiavelli |
| *The Witch Cult in Western Europe: the Original Text...* | Margaret Murray |
| *Bankers and Other Rogues: A Brief History...* | Alexander Del Mar |

Obtainable at all good online and local bookstores.
View Aziloth Books' full list at: www.azilothbooks.com

Parchment Books
AZILOTH

www.ingramcontent.com/pod-product-compliance
Lightning Source LLC
La Vergne TN
LVHW010103110826
845155LV00028B/467

* 9 7 8 1 9 1 1 4 0 5 6 2 7 *